founde. ... apy. She works both for
the NHS and foi ... ve Therapy Centre. Through ten years of
clinical research with the University of Oxford, she helped to develop and
evaluate cognitive behavioural treatments for social phobia and for
generalized anxiety disorder. She has a special clinical interest in the use
of CBT during recovery from traumatic experiences in childhood and runs
training workshops on a wide variety of topics relevant to practitioners of
CBT, in the UK and other countries. She is particularly interested in
making the products of research available to the general public and, in
addition to being the author of *Overcoming Social Anxiety and Shyness*, she
is co-author of *Manage Your Mind: The Mental Fitness Guide* and of
Psychology: A Very Short Introduction.

The *Overcoming* series was initiated by PETER COOPER, Professor of
Psychology at the University of Reading and Honorary NHS Consultant
Clinical Psychologist. His original book on bulimia nervosa and binge-
eating founded the series in 1993 and continues to help many thousands
of people in the USA, the UK and Europe. The aim of the series is to help
people with a wide range of common problems and disorders to take
control of their own recovery programme using the latest techniques
of cognitive behavioural therapy. Each book, with its specially tailored
programme, is devised by a practising clinician. Many books in the *Overcoming* series are now recommended by the UK Department of Health
under the Books on Prescription scheme.

Other titles in the *Overcoming* series:

3-part self-help courses

Single-volume books

OVERCOMING
SOCIAL ANXIETY
AND SHYNESS
SELF-HELP COURSE

A 3-part programme based on
Cognitive Behavioural Techniques

Part Three: Putting It All Together

Gillian Butler

ROBINSON
London

Constable & Robinson Ltd
3 The Lanchesters
162 Fulham Palace Road
London W6 9ER
www.overcoming.co.uk

First published in the UK by Robinson,
an imprint of Constable & Robinson Ltd 2007

A copy of the British Library Cataloguing in
Publication Data is available from the British Library.

Important Note
This book is not intended as a substitute for medical advice or treatment.
Any person with a condition requiring medical attention should consult
a qualified medical practitioner or suitable therapist.

ISBN: 978-1-84529-443-4 (Pack ISBN)

ISBN: 978-1-84529-571-4 (Part One)

ISBN: 978-1-84529-572-1 (Part Two)

ISBN: 978-1-84529-573-8 (Part Three)

Printed and bound in the EU

1 3 5 7 9 10 8 6 4 2

Contents

Note to Practitioners

This self-help course is suitable for a wide range of reading abilities and its step-by-step format makes it ideal for working through alone or with help from a friend or professional. The course is divided into three workbooks, and each contains a full supply of worksheets and charts to be filled in on the page – so there is no need for photocopying. If you do decide to photocopy this material you will need to seek the permission of the publishers to avoid a breach of copyright law.

Introduction: How to Use this Workbook

This is a self-help course for dealing with social anxiety and shyness. It has two aims:

1 To help you develop a better understanding of the problem

2 To teach you the practical skills you will need in order to change.

How the course works

The *Overcoming Social Anxiety and Shyness Self-Help Course* will help you understand how social anxiety and shyness develop and what keeps them going, and then to make changes in your life so that you begin to feel more confident.

These workbooks are designed to help you work, either by yourself or with your healthcare practitioner, to overcome social anxiety and shyness. With plenty of questionnaires, charts, worksheets and practical exercises, the three parts together make up a structured course.

It is important to be realistic: doing these tasks is time-consuming and sometimes difficult; it can also be rather repetitive. The key point to remember is that the exercises and worksheets are ways of working that research has shown to be helpful for many people. You could adapt the exercises to suit yourself, or change them from time to time if that makes the tasks more interesting.

Part One explains:

- What social anxiety is

- What are its symptoms and effects

- The different kinds of social anxiety and how common it is

- What shyness is and how it links with social anxiety

- How the way you think plays a major role in social anxiety

- What causes social anxiety

- What happens when you are socially anxious – and pinpointing what needs to change.

Part Two explained:

- Some general ideas about overcoming social anxiety

- How to reduce your self-consciousness

- How to change your thinking patterns

- How to do things differently.

This part, Part Three explains:

- How to build up confidence

- How to deal with underlying beliefs and assumptions

- How to put what you've learnt into action and overcome any practical problems

- How to become more assertive

- How to overcome bullying in your past

- How to develop relaxation skills

Working through this part will help you feel more assured, more comfortable and more at ease with yourself.

How long will the course take?

Each workbook will take at least two or three weeks to work through – but do not worry if you feel that you need to give each one extra time. Some things can be understood and changed quite quickly, but others take longer. You will know when you are ready to move on to the next workbook. Completing the entire course could take two or three months, but it could take less and it could take a lot more. This will depend on the level of your social anxiety, on how quickly you are able to work and how ready you feel to make changes in your life. Take your time, and go at the pace that suits you best. You are the best judge of what you can do at any one time. If you get stuck and need a break from the work, make sure you plan when to start again.

Getting the most from the course

Here are some tips to help you get the most from the workbooks:

- These workbooks are not precious objects to be kept on the shelf – they are practical tools. So feel free not only to write on the worksheets and charts, but also to underline and highlight things, and to write comments and questions in the margins. By the time you have finished with a workbook it should look well and truly used.

- You will also find lots of space in the main text. This is for you to write down your thoughts and ideas, and your responses to the questions.

- Keep an open mind and be willing to experiment with new ideas and skills. These workbooks will sometimes ask you to think about painful issues. However, if social anxiety is distressing you and restricting your life it really is worth making the effort to do this as it will help you to overcome it. The rewards will be substantial.

- Be prepared to invest time in doing the practical exercises – set aside 20 to 30 minutes each day if you can.

- Try to answer all the questions and do the exercises, even if you have to come back to some of them later. There may be times when you get stuck and can't think how to take things forward. If this happens don't get angry with yourself or give up. Just put the workbook aside and come back to it later when you are feeling more relaxed.

- You may find it helpful to work through the workbooks with a friend. Two heads are often better than one. And if your friend also suffers from social anxiety you may be able to encourage each other to persist, even when one of you is finding it hard.

- Use the Thoughts and Reflections section at the back of the workbook to write down anything that has been particularly helpful to you. This can be anything you read (here or elsewhere), or think, or do, or anything that someone else says to you. These pages are to help you collect together your own list of helpful ideas.

- Re-read the workbook. You may get more out of it once you've had a chance to think about some of the ideas and put them into practice for a little while.

- Each workbook builds on what has already been covered. So what you learn when working with one will help you when you come to the next. It's quite possible simply to dip into different ones as you please, but you will get most out of this series of three workbooks if you follow them through systematically, step by step.

A note of caution

These workbooks will not help everyone who has problems with social anxiety and shyness. Everyone finds it hard to turn and face a problem that troubles them and doing so can make you feel worse at first. However, a few people find that focusing on social anxiety persistently makes them feel worse instead of better. This might be because they have another problem as well. The most common problems that go with social anxiety are depression and dependence on alcohol (or non-prescribed drugs). The recognized signs of clinical depression are listed below. They include:

- Constantly feeling sad, down, depressed or empty
- General lack of interest in what's going on around you
- A big increase or decrease in your appetite and weight
- A marked change in your sleep patterns
- Noticeable speeding up or slowing down in your movements and how you go about things
- Fatigue, and feeling low in energy
- An intense sense of guilt or worthlessness
- Difficulty concentrating and making decisions
- A desire to hurt yourself or a feeling that you might be better off dead

If you have become depressed because of your social anxiety, and the depression is getting in the way of using this workbook, then it would be sensible to deal with the depression first. However, many people who feel a bit depressed from time to time find that the constructive work on solving their underlying social anxiety problem also makes them feel less unhappy.

If you have had five or more of the symptoms listed above (including low mood or loss of interest) for two weeks or more, you should seek professional help from a doctor, counsellor or psychotherapist. There is nothing shameful about seeking this sort of professional help – any more than there is anything shameful about taking your car to a garage if it is not working as it should, or going to see a lawyer if you have legal problems. It simply means taking your journey towards self-knowledge and self-acceptance with the help of a friendly guide, rather than striking out alone.

SECTION 1: Building Up Confidence

This section will help you to understand:

- Where confidence comes from

- The difference between confidence and self-confidence

- How to behave as if you're confident

- How to become more socially active.

One of the qualities that virtually everyone who's ever suffered from social anxiety most desires is confidence. With confidence, we believe, we can do almost anything. But what is confidence, where does it come from and how can we build it up? Let's explore this in detail in this section.

Where does confidence come from?

Many people assume that confidence is something that you either have or don't have. Either you have inherited a strong personality from your parents, or your confidence was written in the stars. But, as we'll see, this assumption is wrong.

Another common assumption is that confidence comes from experience; from the things that happened to you and from the way you were treated as you grew up. Many people believe that you have everything necessary for confidence if, for example:

- The people around you were helpful and appreciative, and did what they could to encourage your development

- They were not too harsh in their criticism or punishment, and built you up rather than undermined you

- You fitted in well at school and were able to make friends.

If these things didn't happen, many people believe, then the opportunity for becoming confident has been missed once and for all. But this is not true either.

As we saw in Part One, Section 6, page 68, many factors combine to make you the way you are. Whatever your age, and whatever your life-story, your self-confidence can still increase.

Your confidence depends on what you're doing

There are some facts about confidence that it might be useful to know. First, there are many different ways in which someone can be confident, or unconfident. Someone might be confident that she can cook a good meal for a family celebration, but unconfident that she can learn to use a computer program for drawing diagrams.

A shy or socially anxious person might have no problem with various demanding activities, like climbing a mountain, or being able to set up an accounts system, but still find it difficult to enter a room full of people.

So the degree of confidence that you feel is not fixed, but depends on what you are doing. Beware of thinking of yourself as unconfident as a person. Try instead to divide your confidence up into its different parts; the things you are confident about doing and the things you are not so confident about. That way you'll reduce your sense of being generally inadequate and develop a sense of your talents and strengths being varied and more complex.

Here are some examples of the many, non-social, activities that contribute to feeling confident.

- Being able to drive a car, or cook a meal, or plan a holiday.

- Choosing what you like in the way of music, or pictures, or plays; TV programmes, or films; books to read; sporting activities; hobbies, e.g. gardening, photography, making a collection.

- Skills: playing a sport, or musical instrument, or making things, or using a computer or word processor.

- Running things: a house, or a club or a business.

- Working skills: organizing yourself, planning your day, managing your time efficiently.

- Keeping your financial or tax affairs in order.

- Using your knowledge: identifying plants, or cars, or antiques; doing crosswords; improving your home.

Make a list here of some of the things you are confident about doing.

_____

_____

_____

_____

_____

_____

Is self-confidence different from this?

This is a difficult question to answer. People who are not self-confident talk as if they have a general lack of confidence. Here are some of the ways they describe themselves as behaving. You might want to place a tick beside any statement you relate to:

☐ 'I am very uncertain or tentative in the way I approach things.'

☐ 'I am reluctant to try anything new or to show initiative.'

☐ 'I feel uncertain and doubtful before, during or after doing something I find difficult.'

☐ 'I seek reassurance from others.'

☐ 'I want to keep my weaknesses well hidden.'

Many people say their lack of self-confidence makes them feel inadequate or inferior or incompetent compared to the people around them. They also believe other people do not have similar doubts. It's as if lacking self-confidence sets them apart from other people, and makes them different.

But even if you believe you have no self-confidence at all, there will still be some things that you feel confident about. The problem is that you may undervalue, ignore or discount these things. You may see them as unimportant and of no significance.

You might be able to read a map, or keep small children amused for an afternoon, or keep your potted plants alive throughout the winter, or install a new computer program; but you don't consider these things as important. You may discount them as if they had no personal meaning, and assume that your kind of 'unconfidence' is somehow more basic.

Confidence isn't fixed

Confident people also have doubts about themselves. The amount of confidence that self-confident people feel at any particular time is not fixed and constant even if that's how it may seem to you.

Someone's sense of self-confidence does not depend only on what they are doing. It also depends on things such as their general attitudes about what matters, and their moods; on how they are feeling. At low moments, when they feel dispirited or tired or lacking in energy and initiative, the feeling of confidence may seem to ebb away. Sometimes it springs back as soon as the feeling changes for the better, and sometimes it is slow to return.

Anyone's confidence can take a jolt, for instance:

- If they suffer a painful rejection

- After an apparently endless run of bad luck

- After making a mistake that they 'should have been able to foresee'.

Confidence ebbs and flows, and this means that everyone, confident people included, sometimes worries about things that normally would hardly bother them.

Ways to look confident

We've seen that many people – even most people – can look confident even when that is not how they feel. Some people consciously adopt an image of confidence, and then they can, for example, introduce their partner to a colleague even when they feel nervous.

Other people assume, unconsciously perhaps, that, even if they 'do it badly', it will not really matter. So they might stumble over words, or make an introduction in an awkward way, but not let this bother them too much. They can allow it to flow out of the mind like water flows down a river. They go on to the next thing without dwelling too much on the temporary embarrassments that happen to everyone.

Behaving 'as if'

When you put on the veneer of confidence, then people tend to take you at face value. They assume that you are as confident as you look. This is one reason why socially anxious people often suppose that they are less confident (and less competent) than others. They are aware of what lack of confidence feels like inside and they cannot easily tell how unconfident other people feel. It is also why one of the most useful and helpful strategies to adopt is to behave 'as if' you were more confident than you feel.

For any social situation you find difficult ask yourself how you would behave if you really were confident. It might be when joining a conversation for instance. Or when you are about to enter a room full of people and feel like sliding invisibly through the door. Let's look at Ruth's story for some ideas.

CASE STUDY: Ruth

Ruth is 42 and has suffered from social anxiety all her life. Her particular difficulty at work is expressing her opinion at meetings. She blushes as soon as she opens her mouth, becomes very conscious about every sentence that enters her head and agonizes over what her colleagues must think of her awkwardness and inability to say what she thinks. Her fears make her sit low in her seat during meetings, eyes focused down on the paper in front of her. The most she has ever contributed is a nod of the head or murmured, 'yes' when other people express their view.

After working with her therapist Ruth decided to change her whole style and approach at her next departmental meeting. Although it was difficult she tried to treat the exercise like an audition for a film in which she had the part of a confident career woman. She thought a lot about how a confident career woman would look and behave in such a meeting.

Ruth decided as a first step she would dress more smartly and boldly than her usual mousey, hideaway style. She also decided a confident career woman would speak clearly so that she could be heard in the meeting and would turn to look at who was speaking throughout the meeting. She would hold her shoulders back and maintain eye contact, generally looking alert and interested.

Ruth practised in front of a mirror at home how she might hold herself and even the way she might speak. Although she felt a little silly at first, after a while she started to enjoy herself.

To her amazement Ruth found the next meeting went much better for her. Although she still blushed when she spoke she decided to ignore how red and hot she felt. Instead she maintained her confident posture with her back straight, shoulders back and eyes meeting other people's gaze. She kept telling herself. 'You're doing well', 'You're handling this okay'. She found that the more she began to offer her opinion the easier it got and that even when people disagreed with what she suggested she could continue to participate.

Now it's time to apply the same lessons to your own life. Begin by describing a situation that you often find difficult.

_____

_____

Now imagine how you would handle this situation if you were confident. Write your answers to the following questions in the space provided and then use your answers to create a new image (or internal video) of yourself in this situation

How would you look?

_____

_____

_____

How would you move?

_____

_____

_____

How would you behave?

_____

_____

_____

How would you stand?

_____

_____

_____

Standing in an upright yet relaxed way, and being ready to meet other people's gaze, for example, changes the whole situation. It helps you to interact in an apparently more confident way, and that in turn has a remarkable effect on how confident you feel.

This is because your behaviour and your feelings link up. The link is obvious when you **feel** anxious and **behave** nervously. But it also works the other way round, when you **behave** confidently and then **feel** better. Behaving the way you want to feel can bring about real change.

Positive thinking

The effect will be even stronger if you give yourself an encouraging message or think confident thoughts as well. Again, if your head is full of self-doubts and negative beliefs you will feel bad and your behaviour will be less confident.

Instead of negative thoughts say something to yourself that reflects the confidence you would like to feel, such as:

- 'It's fine to be the way I am.'

- 'I'm doing OK.'

- 'I want to be friendly.'

- 'None of these people are really out to threaten me.'

Write down your own positive messages to yourself here.

_____

_____

_____

_____

_____

Thoughts such as these may help to bring about the sense of confidence from which everything else follows. Behaving 'as if' these thoughts were true can make a big difference to how you feel, to what you do, and also to what happens to you next. Different behaviour from you can bring about different behaviour from others.

Easier ways to become more confident

Researchers have found that people forget themselves and their anxiety more easily if they are involved in activities that are helpful to others. For example, you could participate in a community project to raise funds for a new playground, or to make access to the local shops easier for disabled people.

Working on a useful project like this helps you to forget yourself more easily. It also provides a sense of belonging that can help to reduce your sense of difference or isolation.

Working together with others on a joint concern eases communication in many ways, whatever the particular cause: political, social, educational, cultural, sporting or of some other kind. You may find that you are able to contribute more easily and feel less shy when you're involved in a cause that you feel strongly about than in other social situations. You will also probably feel more confident about what you have to offer the group.

Joining a cause of particular interest to you could provide the kind of success experience that gives your confidence a real boost. With the boost behind you, it is often easier to tackle something harder that might feel more personally relevant, like asking someone out for a date or speaking up in front of a group.

Make a list here of some of the local causes or groups you are, or possibly could be, interested in.

_____

_____

_____

_____

_____

_____

_____

Being involved with non-threatening people

Doing things with people you find especially unthreatening provides another helpful way to build your confidence. Exactly who you find unthreatening will depend on you. But some possibilities include:

- People younger than yourself, or children
- Older people
- Single people
- People who have young families
- People who live in a certain neighbourhood
- Family members.

Make a list here of some of the sorts of people you don't find threatening and who you could get involved with relatively easily.

_____

_____

_____

_____

_____

_____

The principle is a simple one: success breeds success. If you can seek it out, then you will be able to use it to build up your confidence.

When your confidence doesn't grow

Confidence grows when things go well for you, and it comes partly from doing things that you find difficult, rather than avoiding them or withdrawing from them. The more you do, the more likely it is that your confidence will grow.

However, for some people their underlying beliefs and assumptions persist despite the changes they make and affect their ability to gain social confidence. The next section looks at ways of tackling beliefs and assumptions.

Summary

1 Confidence is not one thing, but many. It develops from experience, and it comes and goes.

2 Even confident people sometimes feel unconfident.

3 You can build confidence by behaving 'as if' you were confident.

4 You can also build confidence by seeking out easier social interactions.

SECTION 2: Underlying Beliefs and Assumptions

This section will help you to understand:

- The different levels of thinking and how they affect confidence

- How to deal with negative beliefs

- How to build more positive beliefs.

First let's take a quick look at the different ways in which we think. This is important for helping you understand why beliefs and assumptions have such powerful effects. We looked at ways of thinking in more detail in Part Two, Section 3, page 44 so you may want to re-read that section as well.

The different levels of thinking

In Part One, Section 5, we saw that there were three levels of thinking we all practise:

1 The level of attention we pay to things

2 The level of our automatic thoughts

3 The level of our underlying beliefs and assumptions (see pages 53–61).

Beliefs

The deepest layer of thinking is the level of our beliefs. These reflect our basic attitudes. Some examples of basic beliefs are:

a 'I can handle most of the things that come my way'

b 'People are usually trustworthy'

c 'Things are bound to go wrong some of the time'.

As these examples show, one way of dividing up the sorts of beliefs that people have is to think of them in terms of whether they apply to yourself (as in example a), to other people (example b) or to the world in general (example c).

Assumptions

Assumptions are like rules for living that fit with your underlying beliefs. They are the ways you put your beliefs into practice in your daily life. Some assumptions that match the sample beliefs we listed above are:

a 'If I was asked to do something new I could probably learn how to do it'

b 'If people are friendly towards you, you can mostly believe what they say'

c 'If things sometimes go wrong, then it is important to remember that they sometimes go right too'.

These examples also show that thinking at any level can be generally positive as well as being generally negative.

Automatic thoughts

At the next level are automatic thoughts. These reflect what comes into your mind from moment-to-moment, whether or not you have put it into words. Automatic thoughts literally 'pop into your head'. Some examples of automatic thoughts are:

a 'This is going to be difficult'

b 'He was really friendly to me'

c 'This is about to go horribly wrong'.

Level of attention

At the level of attention are all the things that we notice and pay attention to. If you are socially anxious these may be things such as your internal feeling of dread and sense of hesitation, self-consciousness and your glimpses of other people's yawns or frowns.

How the three levels fit together

These three levels of thinking fit together. This is how they combine for Eric, an extremely shy 52-year-old.

Eric **believed** that other people were mostly hostile.
He **assumed** he should 'never let his armour drop'.

He **thought** that people were always looking for ways to put him down.
And he **noticed** their failure to smile or say 'good morning' to him.

And here is how it worked for Donna, a socially anxious 23 year-old:

Donna **believed**, underneath, that 'People are usually critical and rejecting'.
She **assumed** that 'If you meet someone new, you should be wary of them, and keep on your guard'.
She **thought** 'They don't like me'.
And she **noticed** her nervousness when she met strangers.

The point of emphasizing this idea here is that when negative beliefs and assumptions dominate your thinking, or are especially powerful, they can continue to influence your thinking and what you notice. This happens despite your best efforts to change your thinking patterns, your behaviour and your self-consciousness as described in Part Two.

When your negative beliefs and assumptions are this strong they need special attention.

Where do beliefs and assumptions come from?

People are not born with their beliefs ready made. Your beliefs are more like conclusions that you have come to on the basis of what happened to you. Thinking patterns develop over many years. If you have had long-standing difficulties that affected your social life, you may have very strong and very negative beliefs and assumptions.

CASE STUDY: Philip

Philip is 37 and single. He very much wants to meet a nice woman and settle down but finds it difficult to talk to attractive women or to socialize generally. During therapy Philip came to examine more closely his underlying beliefs and assumptions. He had powerful memories of being punished severely and unpredictably as a child. He came to believe, early in his life: 'I am always doing things wrong', and developed a rule for living to go with this belief: 'If you keep out of the way, you will also keep out of trouble.'

While he was growing up Philip's belief made sense, based as it was on his direct experience. His rule for living that went with his belief also served a useful function. 'Keeping out of the way' as a child prevented him from being unpredictably punished.

However, Philip had begun to realize that his 'keeping out of the way' rule was not such a useful rule later on in life. It was directly preventing him from joining in social activities, talking to people, making new friends, and in particular, forming a more intimate relationship. Philip realized that powerful as his rule for living was, he needed to work on changing it.

Just like Philip's, your 'old' beliefs may be outdated. The methods we look at next will help you to update and revise those of your beliefs that get in the way of change. They will help you to develop new rules for living that work better for you now.

Often we do not know where the beliefs and assumptions that we have ended up with came from. But sometimes they seem to have developed after particular distressing events, like being teased and rejected at school, being harshly criticized, or feeling humiliated and embarrassed in front of people whose opinion was important. Someone who was teased or bullied at school might well come to hold a belief such as 'I am unacceptable'. This belief could persist until it is brought out into the open and re-examined.

Such experiences can seem like strong evidence for your beliefs at the time, and leave you with painful memories or images. But these experiences do not prove that your beliefs are generally true.

When beliefs and assumptions like these prevent you making progress, it is important to learn to step back and take a cool look at them. Think about them again, as if from a completely different standpoint, and see them as someone else might see them. Ask yourself the following questions:

- The belief may once have seemed to be true, but is it now outdated?

- Is the belief exaggerated?

- Is anybody totally unacceptable, for instance?

- Is your belief more like a feeling – based on unpleasant, distressing memories – than a thought based on hard fact?

We'll provide exercises to help you identify and challenge your beliefs later in this section but for now let's look more closely at how beliefs work in your day-to-day life.

How beliefs and assumptions work

Our beliefs and assumptions provide the framework with which we approach the world. It is as if everything that happens to us, everything we see, think and involve ourselves in, has to be sifted through this filter on its way in.

Imagine that the way in which all of us filter the information that comes to us is like a window on the world. Then the shape of that window, and the colour of the glass in it, and where we stand in relation to it, determine what we see.

If the window is too small, or has coloured, dirty or uneven glass in it, then it will limit or distort what we can see. If we could look through another window instead – or come closer so that we could see out properly, or open it wide so that we did not have to peer through the glass – then we would see things differently.

All of these actions would give us a new perspective. But most of us assume that our view of the world is realistic. We do not stop to think about the characteristics of the window we may be looking through. Instead we believe that our view is the correct, or even the only possible, one.

CASE STUDY: Stephen

Stephen is 27 and has a powerful belief that nobody likes him. He was badly bullied at school and that experience has stayed with him into adulthood. When a colleague at work invited him out for a drink Stephen had the following thoughts:

- *'She must have been pushed for company'*

- *'She probably just felt sorry for me'*

- *'Maybe she wants me to do something for her'.*

Later, when he was talking to his therapist about the situation he added, 'Nobody wants me around' – as if the invitation had in fact never happened. From his perspective, the friendliness of the invitation was not even part of the picture. Stephen's window on the world desperately needed cleaning and it was his own negative beliefs that were the problem.

Changing underlying – or undermining – beliefs

Underlying beliefs reflect what things mean to you. They often 'go without saying', and therefore may be hard to put into the exact words that fit for you. They also seem obviously true when you believe them, so that there seems to be no point in questioning them. But this is wrong, as beliefs can be just as false, misguided, unhelpful or outdated as any other kinds of thoughts.

Let's look at some examples of the beliefs of other socially anxious people. These may help you to identify the kinds of beliefs that undermine your confidence. Remember, as we saw in Part One, Section 5, these beliefs may be more like an underlying sense of yourself than a clear statement that you regularly put into words. They also tend to reflect categorical judgments. These are judgments that are supposedly absolutely right or wrong and admit no half-measures.

Here are some examples of negative beliefs. Place a tick beside any you relate to.

☐ 'I am odd'

☐ 'I am weird'

☐ 'I am different'

☐ 'I am boring'

☐ 'I am unattractive'

☐ 'I am inferior'

☐ 'I am inadequate'

☐ 'I am unacceptable'

☐ 'I am unlikeable'.

Negative beliefs reflect your ideas and impressions about how other people are too. Place a tick beside any of the following statements you relate to:

☐ 'Other people are always judging me'

☐ 'Other people are always criticizing'

☐ 'Other people are never unconfident or anxious'

☐ 'Other people don't like people who are nervous'

☐ 'Other people don't like people who are shy'

☐ 'Other people don't like people who are quiet'.

For more information on negative beliefs, see Part Two, Section 3, page 45.

These beliefs often sound – and may feel – like statements of fact. However, in reality they reflect your opinions and attitudes rather than facts. You can question and re-examine your negative beliefs. In time you can also learn how to rephrase them in less harsh or absolute, terms. We look at two straightforward steps for helping you do this next.

Step 1: Identifying your own personal beliefs

Start by thinking of a recent situation in which you felt socially anxious. It is best to have a particular situation in mind (like 'going to Claire's house last week'), rather than a **type** of situation (like 'meeting new people').

Good examples would be situations such as a time when you got angry with someone but could not say so, or a time when you heard the voices of people talking in the room you were about to enter and stopped because you were suddenly flooded with feelings of anxiety and dread.

Philip, the socially anxious 37-year-old we met earlier, wrote:

I was recently anxious when I went to speak to Caroline in Accounts. Actually I wanted to get her into conversation because I like her a lot and I wanted to suggest having lunch together. Instead I couldn't look her in the eye, mumbled something stupid about a work problem and left as soon as I could without having suggested lunch.

Write down a situation that recently made you anxious here.

_____

_____

_____

_____

_____

Now think through this situation from beginning to end. Try not to avoid anything about it that might make you shudder again as you recall it. The idea is to face up to its full implications.

Identifying beliefs and assumptions can be a painful business, so give yourself time and try not to rush into it. Remember that many other people have similar beliefs. You are not the only one who has to work at them in order to feel better, and do the things that you want to do.

Make yourself go through all the details of what happened. You could:

- Describe them to yourself

- Talk yourself through it again

- Imagine that you can see it all on a video or DVD screen.

Pay attention to the thoughts, the general impressions and the images that come to mind. Also focus on anything you remember saying to yourself during the situation such as 'You're not handling this well', 'That was a stupid thing to say' and so on. Focus on what you think you did 'wrong' in that situation. Then answer the following key questions. For each question we've first shown you how Philip answered.

Key questions for identifying beliefs

1 What do you think were your shortcomings?

Philip wrote: *I couldn't look Caroline in the eye and mumbled. And I didn't manage to ask her out. I'm hopeless at speaking to women and they can see I'm an idiot.*

Now write your answer.

_____

_____

_____

_____

_____

_____

2 How are you judging yourself?

Philip wrote: *I see myself as a failure at these basic social interactions. I'm weird and nobody would ever want to go out with me.*

Now write your answer.

_____

_____

_____

_____

_____

_____

3 What did it mean to you? Why was it so difficult and upsetting?

Philip wrote: *It fitted in with what my father used to say about me; that I was hopeless and nothing but trouble, and that it would have been better if I'd never been born.*

Now write your answer.

_____

_____

_____

_____

_____

_____

4 What does it mean about you?

Philip wrote: *I've fulfilled my father's expectations. I'll never amount to anything; no one will want to spend time with me. And a woman certainly wouldn't want to settle down with me.*

Now write your answer.

_____

_____

_____

_____

_____

_____

5 What are the attitudes of others?

Philip wrote: *Other people think I'm weird and a loser.*

Now write your answer.

_____

_____

_____

_____

_____

_____

_____

_____

6   What does this tell you about them?

Philip wrote: *They don't have the sorts of problems I do. They can chat easily to people and ask them out. They're normal and I've got problems.*

Now write your answer.

_____

_____

_____

_____

_____

_____

_____

The aim is to clarify what the situation meant to you then, and what it still means to you – and about you – now. Then, with one of your 'social failures' fully in mind, complete each of these sentences:

I am:

_____

_____

Others are:

_____

_____

_____

Use whatever words come to mind to express your inner beliefs. Your own words will reflect the particular shade of meaning that is important to you. Although many people may have the same kinds of beliefs, for example about not being likeable, or acceptable, or attractive, they will express them in different ways. These slight differences reflect their different personalities and experiences.

Philip wrote: _'I am a loser and weird. Others are normal.'_

Core beliefs

You could broaden your understanding of yourself and your underlying beliefs by thinking through other difficult or embarrassing events that have happened to you as well. You may find that you always come to the same conclusions, or you may find that you have a relatively large set of beliefs, and that different ones come to the fore at different times.

For example, Philip found in certain situations he strongly believed 'I am always doing things wrong'. In other situations he found he strongly believed 'I am a loser and weird.'

If this is the case for you, ask yourself whether one of the beliefs is more important or more fundamental to you than the others. More fundamental beliefs, or core beliefs, tend to be ones that arouse the strongest feelings, and are most closely related to your worries and fears. They are the ones that make you want to protect yourself most, and to seek out ways of keeping yourself safe. This is because facing up to them and to their implications is especially painful. Nobody wants to come to the considered conclusion, like Philip, that 'I'm a loser and weird', for instance. This is harder still if the conclusion reflects an even more fundamental judgment about yourself, such as: 'I'm not the sort of person people can like.'

Write down here any belief that you think might be a core belief.

_____

_____

_____

_____

_____

_____

_____

_____

_____

_____

It is very important to remember that categorical beliefs such as this are extremist statements (see Part Two, Section 3, page 68), and they are not likely to be supported by the facts. They are also changeable. But you cannot change them without knowing what they are.

If identifying the belief makes you feel worse, or much worse, try to console yourself with the thought that the bad feelings will not last. The worse you feel the more likely it is that you have succeeded in identifying the crucial beliefs for you. **That does not make the beliefs true:** it just makes it more important that you learn how to re-examine, and modify them.

It's worth remembering...

Deeply upsetting feelings and bad memories do not make negative beliefs about yourself true.

Step 2: Changing beliefs

The second step is to re-examine these beliefs, and to separate the facts from the opinions. This is exactly what we did in Part Two, Section 3, page 46, where we looked at changing other kinds of negative thinking patterns.

However true they seem at first, such categorical beliefs are very likely to be exaggerations or over-generalizations, and they should certainly be questioned.

Look again at the core beliefs you have listed above. Now answer the questions opposite.

Key questions for changing beliefs

1. Would you judge someone else who felt like you do in the same way? What would you say to someone else who held a belief like this one?

2. Are you being fair to yourself?

3. Are you going in for 'character assassination', rather than sticking to what happened on one particular occasion? List some occasions when you behaved differently.

4. Are you forgetting that everyone makes mistakes, gets things wrong, and feels socially uncomfortable at times? That no one can be perfect? Describe some occasions where you have seen other people act awkwardly or when they have told you later they felt embarrassed or shy.

5. Are you ignoring your strengths and focusing on your weaknesses? Ignoring the successes and friendships, while focusing on failures and embarrassments? List some of your successes here.

6. Are you falling into a biased pattern of thinking? Catastrophizing? Taking things personally? Mind-reading? Emotional reasoning? (See the list in Part Two, Section 3, page 54.)

7. Are you drawing conclusions on the basis of your childhood or adolescent experiences?

8. Are you judging yourself as you have (once) been judged? If so, what makes the person, or people, who judged you right now? Who is the best authority on you? Other people or yourself?

The easiest way to practise this work is to use one of the thought records we introduced in Part Two, Section 3. Blank versions are at the back of Part Two. Write the specific situation when you felt anxious or upset in column 1. Next write down your belief in the column for upsetting thoughts. In column 3 list the possible alternatives that challenge this negative belief. In column 4 note any change in the way you feel after you've challenged the belief. Write it as a number from −10 to +10, where −10 means you feel much worse and +10 means you feel much better. In the last column list what you would do differently in a similar situation in future. Philip's first entry is shown on page 26 as an example to help you get started.

Dramatic changes

Questioning underlying beliefs can occasionally have dramatic effects. This happens when it is immediately obvious that the 'old' belief is so exaggerated or so extreme or so outdated that it must be false.

CASE STUDY: Simon

Simon, 33, had been bullied and tormented while he was at school. He had subsequently done his best to keep out of sight and therefore out of mind. He didn't want to be noticed or to stand out in a crowd. That way he couldn't be the butt of anyone's jokes or victimization.

Simon realized when answering the questions for changing negative beliefs that one of his basic beliefs was 'Everyone out there wants to pick on me'. As soon as he started to question this belief he realized that, although it had seemed true once, it was now false. No one had really picked on him for years.

But the fear that they might do so was still there, and because the belief had not been brought out into broad daylight and given proper consideration it was still affecting his behaviour. Although Simon changed his negative belief quickly, it took longer to change his behaviour.

Simon decided to change all the ways, large and small, in which he had learned to keep himself out of sight – and this was hard work. The behaviour patterns that went with the belief that people would always pick on him were second nature by the time he had left school. As an adult he hardly noticed when they occurred.

For example, he never – if he could help it – made a suggestion or asked anyone a question; and he was used to positioning himself behind other people, in the least conspicuous place he could find. He had been doing these things so long that he was no longer aware of doing them.

Although it was fairly easy for him to recognize that his belief was now false, chang-ing still took time and effort. It involved doing things differently – including choosing different, more colourful clothes to wear – as well as changing his outdated patterns of thinking. Working at changing behaviours is important when working on beliefs; other-wise old habits persist, and contribute to maintaining the difficulties.

At times Simon found that doing things in a new way – 'as if' most people would accept him in the normal way – filled him with fear and dread. It took many weeks of determined practice before he felt he was on his way to overcoming his anxieties.

Simon's fear is understandable too. Anyone would feel fearful if they did something they truly believed was risky and threatening. This is the social equivalent of putting your head in the lion's mouth.

But it does not mean that you cannot change, or that trying to change is bad for you and could make you worse. It just means that confronting an old fear brings the fear out into the open, and this is not pleasant.

Why are beliefs so hard to change?

Many people know 'at some level' that their undermining beliefs are not really true, even though they **feel as if** they are. So they might feel inadequate even while know-ing in their rational minds that they are not. This was the case with Simon. When his negative belief came out into the open, 'that everyone picked on him', he could see immediately it just wasn't true. But he had been behaving as if it was true for decades.

This is an example of **emotional reasoning**, and this type of negative thinking pattern is particularly common when long-standing beliefs are undermining your confidence. We looked at the first line of defence against it in Part Two, Section 3, 'Changing Thinking Patterns'. It is useful to start rethinking the beliefs, and distin-guishing the thoughts from the feelings, by working through a few of your difficult situations using the 'thought records' shown on page 26.

However, it is hard to change the framework with which you approach the world, and to rethink your beliefs. It can take a long time to convince yourself that it makes sense to change your mind when your belief has shaped your social sense of yourself for a long time. If you truly believe that you are different or peculiar, and that this makes you unacceptable or inadequate, then it is difficult to see things another way. Everything you do seems at first to fit with the old belief.

Let's now look at some more ways of working on stubborn, long-lasting and undermining beliefs.

Thought record for challenging beliefs

Situation (be specific)	Upsetting thoughts (keep the different thoughts separate)	Possible alternatives (there may be more than one)	Change in feelings (−10 to +10)	Action plan (what would you like to do differently)
Speaking to Caroline in Accounts	I'm hopeless. I'm weird. I'm a loser.	I may not have seemed as awkward as I felt. I may be mind-reading; Caroline didn't actually say I was behaving in an odd way. I may be catastrophizing – Caroline might still like to talk to me; we have had good conversations on other occasions.	A bit better; probably +2 or 3.	Be more relaxed and not give up on a conversation so quickly.

Searching for new information

The first of these ways of challenging long-lasting beliefs involves searching for new information: information that contradicts, or does not fit with, your belief.

All of us tend to look out for, notice and remember information that fits with our beliefs. We tend to miss or not remember information that does not fit with our beliefs. Let's look at some examples of this.

Margaret thinks she is no good at making pastry. What she notices each time Christmas comes round and she has to make the mince pies again is that she cannot remember how to do it without looking it up in a book. She's very aware that she gets very worried about whether she is doing it right. And she remembers from previous years that the end result is never quite up to scratch and can be more like cardboard than pastry.

If you think that you stick out like a sore thumb and that this will make people pick on you then, similarly, you tend to keep on the lookout for danger signs. You notice when other people look at you, or when someone turns a questioning, or supposedly threatening, gaze in your direction.

To start this search for more positive information work through the counter-belief worksheets shown on pages 29, 30 and 31. There are extra worksheets at the back of the book. We've provided some sample completed worksheets because it is often easier to see when someone else's framework for approaching the world needs to be changed than to see that your own framework should be. The first example is based on someone's fear about making a cake and has no (or little) social relevance. We've included it because it shows very clearly how the various steps in the exercise fit together. The second example focuses on a common socially anxious belief, 'I am not acceptable.' If you share this belief the example might be harder to follow so re-read it a few times.

Steps for completing the counter-belief worksheet

Here are the steps to go through. The first five should be completed **before** the event you fear.

Step 1. Write down your belief on the line at the top.

Step 2. Rate how much you believe this now (0–100 per cent where 0 means you don't believe it all and 100 means you completely believe it).

Step 3. Think ahead to a situation that you feel anxious or worried about that relates to this belief and write it down. It's better to think about a future rather than a past situation. This will be more relevant for how powerful your belief is for you now.

Step 4. Make your prediction. Ask yourself, on the basis of your belief, what do you think will happen? This should help you identify the framework provided by your negative thinking pattern.

Step 5. Next, define your search plan: what new information to look out for, so that you can step outside your current negative framework. As you can work out from the examples shown below, this is easier to do if you have made a clear prediction first.

The next two steps, concerning the outcome of your search and your conclusions, can only be filled in after the event.

Step 6. When the event is over, think about what happened, and how that fitted with your expectations and predictions. Summarize your findings, and write down what the search has revealed (the 'adequate' or 'passable' pastry, instead of the tasteless cardboard).

Step 7. Think about the whole exercise, and draw your own conclusions. Try to step outside your usual framework sufficiently to be able to see things afresh. Some key questions you could ask yourself are:

- Has it alerted you to things that you might not otherwise have noticed?

- Has it demonstrated to you how this belief keeps your thinking stuck in a particular pattern?

- Has it disconfirmed any of your predictions or expectations?

Step 8. The last step in this exercise is to think back to your original belief. There are two kinds of changes that you are looking for.

- First, rate the degree to which you believe it now on the same (0–100) percentage scale.

- Secondly, ask yourself if you would like to change your original belief in any way. Useful changes would make your belief less extreme, or less negative.

The more new information you find, the more likely it is that your belief rating will start to shift, as your search weakens that belief's hold on you, but this may take some time. If you have held the belief in question for some years, and have focused more on the things that support it than on the ones that challenge it, then the exercise will be difficult. It is hard to start seeing things in a new way, without the old, familiar framework.

If you can continue to challenge yourself and your beliefs and keep up the search for new information, then belief change will follow by degrees. Philip, who we met earlier, reacted to doing this exercise with the comment: 'I've been thinking like this so long, that I did not even realize that it could be questioned'.

Counter-belief worksheet 1: example

Step 1. Belief: *I'm no good as a cook*

Step 2. How much do you believe this (0–100 per cent)? *80 per cent*

THE FORWARD SEARCH PLAN

Before the event

Step 3. Think of a future situation that will be difficult for you

My husband's birthday, when I will have to make him a birthday cake and all the family will be there.

Step 4. Your expectation or prediction (this should fit with your belief)

I will not be able to remember how to do it, and will spend hours finding a recipe. I will get in a horrible mess in the kitchen, and something is bound to go wrong. It will fall flat, or be heavy and sticky. Or it will be dry and hard. No one will want to eat it and most of it will be left over.

Step 5. Search plan: What should you be looking out for?

Things I do remember how to do. Being quick to find a recipe. The amount of mess, and the amount of time it takes. What the cake turns out like. How much gets eaten.

After the event

Step 6. Outcome: What actually happened?

Much better than I expected. Found a recipe OK. Did make a horrible mess, but it looked good enough. Also most of them ate it and my daughter said it was good. Someone left a lot but my husband asked for some more the next day.

Step 7. What conclusions can you draw from that?

It's far less clear than I thought it would be: good and bad bits mixed up. Probably over-all not as bad as I predicted, and it tells me I would find it a lot easier if I only did that kind of thing more often.

Step 8. Rethinking your original belief

How much do you believe it now (0–100 per cent)? *40 per cent (At least I could learn how!)*

How would you like to change your belief, now? *I'm not a very good cook … yet.*

Counter-belief worksheet 2: Socially anxious example

Step 1. Belief: *I am not acceptable as I am*

Step 2. How much do you believe this (0–100 per cent)? *65 per cent*

THE FORWARD SEARCH PLAN

Before the event

Step 3. Think of a future situation that will be difficult for you

Having to meet some of my parents' friends at the weekend.

Step 4. Your expectation or prediction (this should fit with your belief)

I will go quiet. I hate small talk, and I can't do it, so there won't be anything to say. I shall feel that I have let them down.

Step 5. Search plan: What should you be looking out for?

Whether other people go quiet too sometimes. Moments when I do have something to say. The kinds of things people talk about. How my parents react to having me there. Whether they say anything that suggests they are disappointed in me.

After the event

Step 6. Outcome: What actually happened?

I felt awful at first, and could only say standard things. But one person asked me about work, and then there was more to say. There were a few moments when everyone was quiet. It certainly wasn't just my fault. Mum is worried about me, being on my own so much. But she was happy about how the event went, so I can't have spoiled it for her.

Step 7. What conclusions can you draw from that?

Saying the 'standard' things did start me off, in the end, and then we got out of the small talk quite quickly. I was lucky that someone asked me about work. I'm certainly not the only one who goes quiet at times. I am probably more worried about letting my parents down than they are. They just want me to be happier.

Step 8. Rethinking your original belief

How much do you believe it now (0–100 per cent)? *50 per cent*

How would you like to change your belief, now? *It's not acceptable to me to be so anxious, and so much on my own, but being that way doesn't make me unacceptable – at least to my parents and their friends.*

Counter-belief worksheet

Step 1. Belief:

_____

_____

Step 2. How much do you believe this (0–100 per cent)?

_____

THE FORWARD SEARCH PLAN

Before the event

Step 3. Think of a future situation that will be difficult for you

_____

_____

Step 4. Your expectation or prediction (this should fit with your belief)

_____

_____

Step 5. Search plan: What should you be looking out for?

_____

_____

After the event

Step 6. Outcome: What actually happened?

_____

_____

Step 7. What conclusions can you draw from that?

_____

_____

Step 8. Rethinking your original belief

How much do you believe it now (0–100 per cent)?

_____

How would you like to change your belief, now?

_____

_____

Building more positive beliefs

Carrying out a search for new information will help you to modify negative, underlying beliefs. It will also help you to build the firm foundation from which your confidence will continue to grow. Searching for new ways of looking at things, as you reconsider the old framework, also helps you to build more positive beliefs.

Positive beliefs, if they are to be most helpful to you, should be phrased in moderate terms. You need to work out for yourself what kinds of positive beliefs are likely to work for you. Philip settled for the statement:

'I'm a mixture of good, bad and indifferent, much like everyone else.'

Simon, whom we met on page 24, said to himself:

'I'm OK as I am. It's OK to be me.'

Try to find the words to sum up a more positive belief for yourself. You should be looking for a belief that helps you to work against the old, negative way of thinking, and that fits with reality. This means avoiding extremist terms.

None of us is wholly and completely lovable, attractive and acceptable all the time, even though people who love us may accept us totally. Loving and accepting people, when you truly know them, more often means loving and accepting them 'warts and all'. This in turn means that letting people know you 'warts and all' is just letting them know you. It is not letting them 'see through you', or discover your hidden faults and weaknesses in a way that leads inevitably to the end of the relationship.

Write down on the form on the next page some new, positive beliefs. There are extra forms at the back of the book. Every day collect some new information that fits with your new belief. Remember this may be out of sight at first. Keep searching, and it will come into view.

Changing assumptions

We've seen that our beliefs reflect absolute judgments about ourselves and others such as: 'I am useless'; 'People are always judging you'.

Assumptions are like rules for living that are based on beliefs. They affect how we behave on a day to day basis, and they are often expressed using words like 'should', 'must', 'ought', 'have to'. An assumption based on the belief, 'I am useless' might be expressed as: 'I should be able to do the things other people can.'

Building more positive beliefs

New belief 1:

_____

_____

_____

_____

_____

_____

Information that fits with this new belief:

_____

_____

_____

_____

Draft new belief 2:

_____

_____

_____

_____

_____

Information that fits with this belief:

_____

_____

_____

_____

_____

If ... then

However, when it comes to changing assumptions, it is most useful to put them into a particular form of words called 'if ... then ...' statements. So the assumption, 'I should be able to do the things other people can' would become, '**If** I try to do something other people can, **then** I will fail.'

When you express an assumption in the 'if ... then' format you can more easily see how your assumption directly influences what you do as well as the way you are likely to think and feel. In the example above, the assumption would make you not try to do many of things other people do (like speaking up in a meeting, for example) because you believe you will fail.

An unhelpful assumption frequently made by people who are socially anxious is: '**If** people knew what I was really like, **then** they would reject me.' This assumption would make it hard to meet new people and it would get in the way of letting people see 'the real you', and of being yourself.

Another common assumption is: 'If others want to know me they'll let me know.' Someone who lives by this rule is unlikely to take the initiative in contacting people or making new friends.

Assumptions like this get in the way of recovery – they determine what you do. The only way to find out if your assumption is incorrect – or indeed correct – is to start taking the initiative. So changing assumptions involves doing things differently.

Try writing down your thoughts about the questions below. And remember, it's useful to try to express your assumption in the 'If…then' format. For example, do you assume that if something goes wrong, **then** it must be your fault?

What assumptions do you make about yourself?

_____

_____

_____

_____

_____

_____

What assumptions do you make about others?

_____

_____

_____

_____

_____

_____

And about who is responsible for the success or failure of your social encounters?

_____

_____

_____

_____

_____

Changing your behaviour

Identifying your assumptions will tell you how to try to change your behaviour. The new behaviour should remove the disadvantages of your old, socially anxious behaviour. It involves taking a risk, and will certainly not feel safe at first. However, it provides another way of challenging the underlying belief that you need to keep yourself safe from potential harm.

Once you truly realize that protective behaviours of all kinds do not really work, then you will find that you can let them go, and 'be yourself'.

Here are the steps to follow.

Step 1: Identify the behaviour that fits with the assumption

This is the 'old behaviour' that reflects how you put the rule for living into practice. Ask yourself, what does this assumption or rule make me do? How do I behave so that I do not break this rule?

For example, Bill believed he was likely to be rejected and took great care to hide from others what he was really like. He said very little and avoided people and social situations. But this undermined his confidence as he became increasingly isolated and lonely.

Step 2: Do something differently

It follows that one of the most effective ways of changing your assumptions is to change your behaviour. Choose a new behaviour that allows you to break the old rule, and to rethink your assumption. You could do this in an easy way first, and build up to harder ways later.

Only if you experiment with doing things differently, and try a new way of behaving, such as letting people know what you are really like, will you be able to find out if the assumption is correct.

Step 3: Look at what happens

Assess what happens when you behave differently. Try to step outside your old framework once again. Think about:

- How things went

- What it means about you that you could choose a new way of behaving

- What it would mean to you if you could go on like this until you felt more confident.

Challenging assumptions in action

Let's look at Simon's exercise to challenge his assumptions.

- Simon's assumption: *'If you disagree with people they will never accept you.'*

- Old behaviour: *Always agree. Keep your opinions to yourself.*

- New behaviour: *Try saying what you think.*

- Evaluation: *The conversation flowed more easily and led to an interesting discussion.*

Write down here some of the ways in which you could behave differently in order to challenge your assumptions. We've left space for you to challenge three of your assumptions. You'll find extra space at the back of the book. Note that the 'Evaluation' section can't be filled in before you have tried out the new behaviour, so this exercise helps you to work both on what you think and on what you do.

Challenging your assumptions

Assumption:

_____

_____

Old behaviour:

_____

_____

New behaviour:

_____

_____

Evaluation:

_____

_____

Assumption:

_____

_____

Old behaviour:

_____

_____

New behaviour:

_____

_____

Evaluation:

_____

_____

Assumption:

_____

_____

Old behaviour:

_____

_____

New behaviour:

_____

_____

Evaluation:

_____

_____

Many assumptions can be phrased in two ways: either in terms of what you should do, or in terms of what you should not do. For example, if you assume, or live by the rule that saying what you think will lead to conflict, this could be worded either in this way:

'If I say what I think then there will be an argument'

or in this way:

'I will get on better with people if I never disagree with them.'

Challenging this assumption follows the same principles, whichever form it takes. Once you start challenging you may get very different results. For example, you might discover that your fear of conflict has led you to:

- Exaggerate the dangers of disagreements

- Underestimate your ability to handle conflict

- Underestimate your ability to handle the strong feelings when conflict arises.

Obeying rules for living such as this one means that disagreements and conflicts are avoided. This deprives you of experiences that could be helpful. In the end confidence is more likely to come from accepting that disagreement and conflict are inevitable, facing up to them when they occur, and learning how to handle them when they do. (If this is a particular difficulty for you, you may find the ideas summarized in Part Three, Section 1 helpful.)

It is true that expressing opinions may reveal differences between people. But avoiding the expression of these differences, or protecting yourself from having to face them, makes them seem worse than they otherwise would. It is the beliefs and assumptions that make it seem best to avoid 'disasters' and to protect yourself from risks. Changing the beliefs and assumptions helps to de-catastrophize such unpleasantness.

A flashcard, to help you remember the main points

It could be useful to make yourself a flashcard (see Part Two, Section 3, page 77) as a reminder of the main points from this section. Flashcards are especially helpful when trying to remember new ways of thinking.

On one side of the card you should write one of your beliefs or assumptions. On the other you should summarize your new ways of thinking. You could include:

- Reminders of any of the confidence building ideas that have come from reading this section

- Any new information that comes from your searches, or from doing things differently

- Any ideas or images that came to mind as you read and that you would like to remember.

Philip drew some windows on the back of a flashcard, to remind himself about the different perspectives that can come from different places, and from looking through different kinds of glass. What this meant to him was: 'Maybe I have been wrong in my beliefs. Maybe there is another way of seeing things. Maybe it is worth going on looking, and trying out doing things differently.' A complicated message can be summarized in a few brief symbols.

Summary

1 Underlying beliefs and assumptions can undermine confidence. They provide the framework within which you see the world, or the window through which you view it.

2 They developed during a lifetime of experience, and they can be changed.

3 There are two main steps for changing beliefs: first you need to identify them, so that you know what they are; then you need to re-examine them.

4 To do this, you will need to step outside the old framework, and search for new information.

5 Building up more positive, helpful beliefs also gives your confidence a surer foundation.

6 So does changing the assumptions that go with your beliefs. This involves changing old patterns of behaviour as well as old patterns of thinking.

SECTION 3: Putting It All Together

This section will help you to understand:

- How the different strategies for overcoming social anxiety fit together

- Some useful general principles

- How other people can help you

- How to deal with common difficulties that may arise when you start to change.

You are probably reading this book because you have suffered from shyness or social anxiety for some time. When a problem persists it is hard to see where to begin when you want to change it. If you would like to use some of the ideas you have read about so far, then you have already made a step in the right direction.

If not, stop and think for a minute.

- What are your doubts and reservations?

- Does it all sound too complicated?

- Do you wonder if you could ever do any of the things described?

- Do you think that people who can use these ideas probably have a mild problem? Yours is too deep-seated to respond to the suggestions made here.

These sorts of thoughts are common. If this is what you think, then you probably feel discouraged too, and find it hard to imagine things being any different.

Remember that there may be another way of seeing things. Challenge your thoughts about being able to change in the same way you have learnt to challenge other negative thoughts.

How would you find out if you could overcome your wish to keep yourself safe? Or whether you could divert your attention away from your sense of embarrassment and distress when you feel self-conscious? Probably only by 'trying and seeing'. This chapter provides some ideas that will help make this easier to do and help you to get the most out of helping yourself.

Let's begin with a reminder of the key strategies we've looked at so far.

Summary of strategies for overcoming social anxiety

All the strategies we've worked through are designed to help you to break the vicious cycles that keep social anxiety going. They are not 'simplistic', or superficial and they all take some time to learn. You have to learn what to do before you can use them effectively.

Don't expect your anxiety to vanish overnight, and remember that social anxiety is a normal part of life. Most people would feel anxious if they were going for an interview, or if they were publicly criticized, or unexpectedly asked to speak at an important meeting or at a friend's wedding. Nothing you can do will get rid of all social anxiety. But you can learn to overcome the anxiety that interferes with your life, or restricts you, and to keep that anxiety within manageable bounds.

Reducing self-consciousness

Self-consciousness comes from focusing your attention on to yourself. This makes you increasingly aware of uncomfortable sensations, feelings, thoughts and behaviours. Consciously focusing on people and things outside yourself instead allows the distress to die away and keeps you more in touch with what is happening around you.

Changing thinking patterns

This method is designed to help you to recognize and to re-examine the way you think. Remember, the fear in social anxiety focuses on your ideas about what other people think about you; on the fear that you will be 'found wanting', or be 'found out'.

Doing things differently

Fear makes you want to protect yourself, but safety behaviours and avoidance make the problem worse, not better. Although it feels risky, it is better to stop trying to protect yourself in these ways. That is the best way to learn that you do not need to do it.

Building up confidence

Confidence may grow quickly, or it may change more slowly. When it is slow to change, this may be because you need also to work on your underlying beliefs and assumptions. You can use the strategies already described to help you to do this. You can also use some others which help you to step outside your old framework for seeing the world, and search for information that helps you to build a new one.

Remember to keep filling in your worksheets and keeping notes of the changes that you have made, and how you were able to make them. Otherwise you may be tempted to think that your improvements are just temporary, and that when things deteriorate again that you have reverted to type. Recognize that such ups and downs are inevitable, and happen to everyone. Patterns of thinking tend to reassert themselves, just like other old habits. You will have to keep working at them until they die away or are replaced with new ones.

Try not to avoid exercises that you find difficult, or going into situations that make you anxious. Recovery is not possible without experiencing some of the fear and distress that have sent you in search of help. The reward is that, as things change, and your confidence grows, the fear starts to subside.

Some general principles to bear in mind

Don't throw yourself in at the deep end
It is sensible to start with taking small risks. Tackle harder things, which involve a greater degree of risk or threat, once you have built your confidence and know more about how the methods work for you.

When you have had one successful experience, do not leave things there, but try the same thing again, as soon as you can
Consolidate your gains, and remember that the more you do the more likely you will notice a change. Do not give up if this is slow to come at first.

Don't work at the problem in fits and starts
If you do, your progress will follow suit, but your moods and feelings may exaggerate the stops and starts until you feel alternately pleased and cast down, as if you were riding a rollercoaster. Instead, try to keep up a steady push in the right direction, for example for two or three months in the first instance.

Be realistic about the things you decide you will try
Don't decide, in your head or on paper, to do something that in your heart of hearts you know is too difficult, and that you will be most unlikely to be able to do. Success is built upon success, so it doesn't matter how small the success is that you start with. It may be as small as making fleeting eye contact, or remembering to smile at someone in the morning. If it works, and you repeat it often enough to know that there

are occasions when it doesn't work as well as others, then you will be able to move on faster than if you had started with something that gave you a sense of disappointment or failure.

Give each strategy a fair trial
Stick with each one until you are sure you understand how it works for you. That way you are likely to be able to make the most of all of the strategies that you need.

Getting help from other people

Overcoming this kind of problem can be lonely work. You are the only one who knows exactly how you feel, the only one who has to face deciding what to do about the problem, and the only one who can take appropriate action. Many people who are shy or socially anxious deal with the problem on their own either because they don't want to tell others about their difficulties or because they don't know people whom they are able to tell.

Working at it alone can be extremely effective, and if you do that then you will know that when things change you are solely responsible for that change. It can also be helpful, though, to have a friend or supporter who is prepared to help. If that person has the time to read about the problem, that may help them to help you most effectively. Above all, you need their encouragement.

It is more helpful if you tell them what you are trying to do. Then they can ask you if you did it, and they might be able to help you out if you meet with difficulties or get stuck. It is not so helpful if they try to push you harder than you are ready to go, or if you rely on them to come with you whenever you have to face something difficult, or to provide a 'quick fix' of reassurance at ever-increasing intervals.

Make a list of the people who you think could help you in your work on overcoming social anxiety.

Some common difficulties

When anxiety seems to 'come out of the blue'

Sometimes symptoms of anxiety can sweep up unannounced, and reach apparently overwhelming proportions when least expected. People often describe this experience as if the anxiety 'came out of the blue', with nothing to set it off or explain it that they can think of.

On careful examination later it usually turns out that there was a link between something that was happening and the symptoms of anxiety, but the link was difficult to find or to understand.

- It may have been that the link was in the meaning of the situation ('this means total rejection again'), rather than in anything specific that happened.

- It could be that a fleeting image popped into your head and encapsulated the meaning of the situation (an image of being humiliated and laughed at).

- A similarity in the situation with earlier distressing events could be the trigger: the sound of someone's voice, the colour of something they are wearing, the smell of the food cooking and so on.

If this happens to you, think first about what the situation means to you, or meant to you. This may give you enough clues to work out the connection. But if you find no connection at all, do not conclude that you are going mad, and losing control of yourself or your feelings.

Try to accept that often we are not able to identify and recognize all the possible connections and links that are there. It is more helpful to accept that there are likely to be some that we will not be able to work out.

When there is nothing you can do about your symptoms

Sometimes there seems no point in telling yourself that you might not tremble or shake because you know that you will. You also know that there is nothing you can do to prevent it, much as you wish that there were.

You will not be able to find in this book any methods that will guarantee that you will not tremble – or indeed suffer from any of the other symptoms of shyness or social anxiety, such as tripping over your tongue and finding that the words you intended to say have come out wrong.

The key to dealing with this difficulty is once again to think in terms of what it means to you when these things happen. If you believe that it means something dire about you, for example that you are inadequate or a useless wreck that no one would want to know, then you may be suffering from the effects of your own, personal (understandable but exaggerated) viewpoint.

The **meaning** of the symptoms rather than the **fact** of the symptoms should once again be the target for change. Using the strategies for changing patterns of thinking, for changing beliefs and for building confidence are the methods that are most likely to be helpful.

When painful memories persist

Some people feel as if memories of the distressing and painful things that happened earlier in their lives keep returning to haunt them. They may have distinct images, or memories or dreams of particular events that recur, bringing at least some of the original distress with them.

It is not easy to lay such memories to rest. However, a few suggestions might be helpful. Researchers have found that if people can communicate about these events and the feelings they had at the time, they start to feel better. This is the case even if you are describing something that happened many years ago and your communication is in writing, or spoken into a tape recorder, rather than made directly to another person. There is something about being able to express oneself that helps to relieve this type of distress.

Use the space below to describe a painful memory that is still causing you problems.

_____

_____

_____

_____

_____

_____

_____

_____

Another strategy that some people have found works for them is to think about what the painful memory means to them, and to develop a new image in their minds that transforms this meaning, and takes away the pain. The idea is to construct a new image, even if it is an unrealistic one, in which your needs at the time that you were most distressed are met in some way.

So the meaning of the new image is that you are comforted, or rescued, or helped or supported or accepted in some way, and the symbolism of the imagery represents this transformation of meaning.

If you would like to try doing this for yourself, you should think about what it was that you needed, or still need, to relieve you of the distress that you feel, and give your mind free play when it comes to imagining how this might come about. Then when the distressing memories return you can consciously call the new image to mind.

Describe here a more positive image, an image in which you are given what you needed to resolve your distress.

When you find it hard to stop the post mortem that can follow an episode of distress

The post mortem makes things worse. It is a way of thinking that brings all the negative biases, attitudes and beliefs into the front of your mind. You then use them to interpret, and even to elaborate upon, the bad side of what actually happened.

The longer a post mortem goes on, the worse it makes you feel. It can sometimes seem increasingly convincing, even though it usually involves a gradual shift away from reality.

There is nothing useful about a post mortem. Despite what some people think, going over in your mind the things that happened, what you said and what other people said, what you both did, the way you looked and felt and so on, does not end in useful conclusions about how to do things better. It provides no valuable clues about how to overcome the problem.

Far better to close down the process as soon as you notice it happening. Distract yourself with something more interesting instead.

When low self-esteem gets in the way

Low self-esteem is different from low self-confidence. It is about your values, and whether you live up to them. It is about your sense that other people value and accept you irrespective of your achievements. And it is about whether you value yourself.

When self-esteem is high, people feel good about themselves. When it is low, people feel bad about themselves, as if they were 'worthless' or did not count, or had nothing to contribute. Then they become inhibited and hold themselves back, and their ability to contribute shrinks a bit.

Low self-esteem is like a particular kind of belief: a belief about yourself and your value, or worthiness. It can be built up in much the same ways as confidence can be built, and using many of the same strategies. If this is a difficulty for you, then it would be best to focus particular attention on identifying your 'self-beliefs'. Try to give words to your low self-esteem, and then work at changing it in the ways described in the previous section. You may also find the *Overcoming Low Self-Esteem Self-help Course* by Melanie Fennell helpful.

Remember that there are no generally accepted yardsticks available for judging the things upon which self-esteem is based. Self-esteem reflects an opinion about you (your own), rather than facts about you, and this opinion may be independent of what other people think.

They may think highly of you despite your own (low) self-esteem; or you may feel that they disapprove of you and reject you, and make you feel that you are different and do not belong, and your self-esteem could still be high.

You may be wrong about their judgements, and using the ideas in this course will help you to discover that they think far better of you than you suppose. Or they may be making a wrong judgement about you, possibly because they do not know you well. If so, as you improve they will have a better chance of discovering their mistake. In either case, it would be a mistake to let other people's opinions, their approval or disapproval, acceptance or rejection, become the measure of your own value.

SECTION 4: Becoming Assertive

This section will help you to understand:

- What assertiveness is
- Why you can't change others but you can change yourself
- How to develop the confidence to say 'no'
- How to learn negotiation skills
- How to deal with criticism, confrontation and conflict.

What is assertiveness?

Being assertive is a way of communicating your needs, feelings or rights to others while being respectful and without infringing their rights. It is easy to understand why people who are shy, or socially anxious, might also find it hard to assert themselves, and to stick up for what they want or what they believe in. This is especially likely to happen when they are confronted with people who have different priorities or beliefs.

Being assertive in part means recognizing that you have some basic rights in any interaction with other people. Read through the checklist below and put a cross against any point you don't agree with.

☐ I have the right to ask for what I want.

☐ I have the right to say 'no' to something I don't want to do.

☐ I have the right to my own opinions, feelings and emotions.

☐ I have the right to make my own decisions.

☐ I have the right to ask for more information or explanation.

☐ I have the right to make mistakes.

☐ I have the right to change my mind.

☐ I have the right to privacy.

☐ I have the right to be independent.

The more points on the list you checked the more likely it is that you will find it help-ful to learn how to become more assertive. This will allow you to express your real self in social situations and interact more fully with other people.

Shyness and unassertiveness

Three kinds of fear are clearly linked to unassertiveness:

1 The fear of being judged, or criticized, or evaluated in negative terms

2 The fear of being rejected or excluded

3 The fear of being seen through and 'found wanting'.

If you are fearful of showing 'weaknesses' then you are unlikely to find it easy to feel that you can meet with others on equal terms, and that makes being assertive diffi-cult. However, some people who find it extremely difficult to be assertive are not socially anxious. And some socially anxious people have few problems being assertive. So although there is an overlap between the two problems they do not always go together.

Much has been written on assertiveness. You can learn about assertive attitudes and skills by reading about them in other self-help books, watching video material or DVDs or attending assertiveness training classes. In this section we're going to look at a few of the specific skills that socially anxious people find particularly use-ful. You will find more ideas on helpful resources at the back of this book.

Balancing passivity and aggression

Assertiveness is based on the idea that your needs, wants and feelings are neither more nor less important than those of other people: they are equally important. This means that you are entitled to your own feelings and opinions, and so is everyone else entitled to theirs. The key assertiveness skills, therefore, help you to:

- Put your ideas and feelings across

- Ensure that your ideas and feelings are given due consideration

- Decide how much weight to give to the feelings and opinions of others.

Other people may want you to feel and to think differently, and you may want them to do the same. But acting upon these 'wants' puts pressure on you or on others to be different – and that is not fair.

The two main traps into which people fall when they behave unassertively are being too passive and the opposite: being too aggressive. Let's look at each of these in turn.

Being passive

Passivity involves going along with others at some personal cost. For example, you might always be the non-drinking, car-driving member of the party because other people assume that you will be, and not because that is what you have chosen. Being passive involves a loss of control, as might happen if other people made decisions that affected you without talking to you first. Passive behaviour, carried to its limits, makes you into a doormat, and as the saying goes, 'If you act like a doormat, don't be surprised if people walk on you'. If you do not speak up, then you may end up doing the job that no one wanted to do, but which everyone else was able to refuse.

Do you think you tend to be too passive in the way you behave? If so, describe a recent situation in which you behaved passively here.

_____

_____

_____

_____

_____

Being aggressive

Of course, there are many reasons why people are aggressive, and many of them have nothing to do with social anxiety, or with being unassertive. However, there is also in some cases an important connection between being – or sounding – aggressive, and being unassertive.

For example, if you do not know how to get people to cooperate with you, or fear that they will not do what you want, then one solution is to use threats. Aggressive behaviour has various advantages for socially anxious people.

- It prevents people getting too close, or keeps them at bay.

- It can be a way of cutting discussion short. If you brook no argument, then you will not have to get into a debate. Aggression tends to bring a speedy end to an interaction.

● It hides fear or pain. It can feel as if it is more acceptable to be aggressive than to be apprehensive or nervous, as aggressive behaviour is more likely to signify strength than weakness in other people's eyes. But the lion – or the lioness – may be more timid than he or she looks.

Do you behave aggressively at times? If so, write about a recent experience here.

_____

_____

_____

_____

_____

_____

Why neither way works

Neither passivity nor aggression is ultimately satisfactory. This is both because of the bad feelings they produce in everyone concerned, and because they are unfair.

For example, James, who allowed the neighbours to borrow his mower whenever they wished, ended with a large repair bill (and many angry unexpressed thoughts). Susan, who made abrupt, burdensome demands on her staff and her family, ended feeling stressed and alienated instead of supported and efficient, which was her aim. To her it felt as if she alone were responsible for getting everything done, which seemed unfair. But she believed asking for help suggested to others that she was weak. That in turn made her feel socially unacceptable: hence her dilemma.

How does being passive or aggressive make you feel? How does it make others feel? Can you identify some of the negative effects of the way you behave? Write them down here.

_____

_____

_____

_____

_____

Being both passive and aggressive

Some people veer between bouts of passivity and bouts of aggression. Or they find that they burst out of periods of passivity as if propelled by an explosive device. Some people who are passive at home are aggressive at work – or the other way round. So you may recognize both patterns in yourself. This introduces one of the main themes of this section: the theme of balance.

It is often difficult, especially when feelings run high, and when opinions differ, to find the middle ground on which to stand up for yourself in a way that does not also put others down. The essence of assertiveness is learning how to do this, with an attitude of fairness: fairness to yourself, as well as fairness to others.

Becoming stuck

Both passive and aggressive reactions to situations lead to 'stuck positions'. Passive people feel that they have no control over the situation, or that they are lacking in social power. Aggressive people feel the opposite: that it is essential to be in control, and to have the power in their own hands.

Assertiveness leads the way out of this impasse by helping people to be more flexible. In this way you can adapt to each other, and feel less at risk of either extreme. Assertive people neither feel controlled nor have the need to control others. Control is altogether less of an issue for them – which is not to say that they do not want their own way as much as everyone else.

Changing yourself, not others

It seems only natural to want to change other people. This is especially the case when you feel that you have been treated unfairly, or dealt an unfair hand. When social anxiety or shyness get in the way, and prevent you standing up for yourself, other people may indeed give you less consideration than they should. Or they may, unfairly, take advantage of you, so that you feel angry, frustrated and resentful.

Socially anxious people may have many reasons for wanting to change other people. The difficulty is that the only person you can change is yourself. It is surprisingly easy to lose sight of this basic fact. If you want people to be different – for example, more friendly, or more considerate of your feelings – then how do you achieve your aim? The only way to do so would be to change yourself: to find ways of making yourself more open to friendship, and ways of expressing your feelings so that others take more notice of them.

Social interactions are like a dance. The steps of one person are matched by those of others. If you change your steps, then those moving with you will be prompted to change theirs too. The changes you make will cause changes in them, so that you can adapt to each other (and vice versa, of course).

If you know how you want to change, then it will be easier to think about how to change your steps in the dance. When you know what you want to achieve, applying the principle of fairness, can help you to build your social confidence as well as your assertiveness.

Having the confidence to say 'no'

Often people who lack social confidence find themselves agreeing to things that they wish they had not agreed to.

- Sometimes they do this because they feel pressured, and give in to others against their better judgement

- Sometimes they do it in order not to offend or displease the person who asked them

- Sometimes it happens because they want to please someone else – for good reasons (wanting to help out a friend) or for less good ones (fear of disapproval).

There are probably other reasons too.

There are three steps to follow when you want to say 'no', but feel tempted to say 'yes':

1   Clarify your priorities

2   Learn the skills of saying no with confidence

3   Be willing to give yourself thinking time.

We'll now look at each of these steps in more detail.

Clarifying priorities

First, decide what you want. Do you, or do you not, want to do as asked? Here are some examples of things other people might ask you to do. Bear them in mind while you work through this section:

- Looking after someone's house plants when they are on holiday

- Taking on an extra commitment to relieve someone else, like your boss or someone in your family

- Tidying the house when visitors are expected

- Making all the practical arrangements for a joint family holiday.

If you can, think of an example from your own experience. Write it down here.

I would like to say 'no' to:

_____

_____

_____

_____

_____

Now think of the cost to you. Think of the time involved. Think of your preferences. Be fair to yourself, and include your likes and dislikes. Write down the problems involved if you say 'yes' here.

The problems in saying 'yes'

_____

_____

_____

_____

Being fair to yourself is not being selfish. It is giving yourself as much consideration as you would give to others. Of course, if you really want to say 'yes', then you will be able to do so without later feeling you have been put upon, or exploited, or taken advantage of. So can you anticipate what you will feel later?

It is only too easy to say 'yes' for the wrong reasons:

- To gain approval from the person who asked you, or to get them off your back

- Because you cannot find an 'acceptable' way of saying 'no'

- To make up for one of your 'perceived' shortcomings.

When you say 'yes' you should, theoretically, be agreeing to something which, given all your priorities, you truly want to agree to. What you agree to should be more important to you than what you have to give up in order to do it. Remember, there is always something that you would be doing instead, even if that is taking the time you need to rest and relax and take stock.

It's worth remembering...

Saying 'no' is not being rude, or uncaring, or uncooperative, or in some other way 'bad'. It is treating your own needs and wishes as equally important as those of others.

This is where the 'shoulds' come in: 'shouldn't' we all go out of our way to help others? Is it not selfish to do what you want when you could be accommodating to others?

This is an important idea, but not one that detracts from the points made about being assertive. If you believe that you should help in the way asked then, at some level, you will want to give that help. You may be reluctant, and busy, or overburdened, or irritated to be asked, but the principle that you believe in – provided you really believe in it – will help you along. However, this is not the only principle that could be involved. Not every request, or expectation, or demand, is one that you 'should' comply with.

Saying 'no' with confidence

If someone asks you to do something that you truly do not wish to do, then all you need to do is to say no. You are under no obligation to explain yourself. You have as much right to say no and to leave it at that as the next person.

However, many people fear that saying no will cause further difficulties for them, such as pressure, confrontation, disapproval or even rejection. They find it easier to say no if they know how to ensure that others will accept their decision.

One way to do this is to find a number of ways to express your decision, and to repeat them calmly and simply, without adding in additional reasons. This is known as the 'broken record' technique. For example, you could say:

- 'No, I am sorry but I can't.'

- 'No, not this time.'

- 'No, I'm afraid not.'

Saying too much when you want to say no and going into elaborate details can make you sound overly apologetic, or as if you are making excuses.

The broken record technique does not always work. This is partly because some people make it hard for us by refusing to take 'no' for an answer. Strategies for saying no with enough confidence to convince others that you mean it can therefore contribute to your sense of fair play. Here are some of the ways of making a refusal easier for someone else to accept, and easier for you to give.

- **Make it clear that you appreciate being asked:** 'Thanks for asking'; 'I appreciate you thinking of me.'

- **Acknowledge the other person's priorities and wishes:** 'I know it is important to you'; 'I understand the difficulty.'

- **Give a clear reason for your refusal:** 'I have to ... visit my grandmother ... complete my tax return ... plan next week's work.'

- **Help the other person to solve the problem,** for example by making a suggestion. Find a balance between dismissing the other person's problem and taking on their problem as if it were your own.

Give yourself time to think

Do you get steamrollered into doing things you do not want to do? Or take on extra commitments out of a sense of misplaced obligation? So often, when people ask us to do things, they also ask for an immediate response, and the sense of time pressure is catching.

But few decisions really have to be made on the spot. A useful response is to say that you will think about it – and of course you also need to find out how long you have in which to think. The point of asking for time is that it helps you to keep things in perspective. It helps you to stand back from the immediate sense of pressure, to take stock, and to work out what you really want, especially when that is not immediately clear to you.

The skills involved in negotiation

Negotiation is only partly about trying to get something that you want. It is also about knowing how to do that fairly: without being aggressive, or manipulative; without moaning or whining or wheedling or demanding.

Most people only start thinking about being in a negotiation at the point of confrontation. They leave it too late. Knowing how to negotiate means that you start off your interactions with other people, both at home and at work, without a warlike, aggressive or defensive attitude. Instead you begin by thinking about how both of you can get what you want – to a degree.

When you are trying to negotiate try to avoid the attitude that if you lose then someone else has won – or, conversely, if you are going to win, then you will have to get the better of someone else. This kind of attitude leads to confrontations, or to arguments, which most shy or socially anxious people go out of their way to avoid. Fear of provoking a confrontation or argument on the one hand, or of being steamrollered on the other, makes it difficult to get what you want. Knowing how to negotiate makes it easier.

Developing a new perspective on negotiation involves rethinking some of these assumptions about winning and losing. An alternative view which leads to much smoother relationships when two people want somewhat different things, is to think instead about the possibilities for mutual gain – a win–win resolution. Then no one has to be a loser, and when your wants and wishes are different from those of the people around you, there is no need to be dominated by the threat of personal loss (or defeat), or by the fear of your own or other people's aggression. The win–win approach works best whether you are negotiating about who does what in the home or about differences of opinion or strategy at work.

Here are some of the principles of cooperation. Negotiations are more likely to succeed, and to create ground for further negotiations later, if they are built upon these principles.

Principles of cooperation

- Think first about what the other person (or people) wants. What is their point of view? If you are not sure, then the first step is to find out. Ask rather than guess.

- Be open about what you want. This may feel risky, but it is one of the quickest ways to build up a sense of mutual trust.

- Do not sidestep the difficult issues. They clarify why negotiation is needed.

- Be prepared to give something up in order to get what you want most. This might open the way to constructive trading between you.

- Keep talking: not in the sense of monopolizing the air time, but in the sense of keeping the door open, so that communication goes on.

- However heated you feel, try not to resort to making personal comments, or slip into the opposite pattern of personalizing remarks that are made to you.

- When responding to someone else, make sure they know that you heard what they said first. Otherwise it is easy to react first and to think later.

Think in terms of building mutual trust.

List here some issues at home or at work you would like to negotiate about:

1 _____

2 _____

3 _____

4 _____

5 _____

Now for each issue write down what you think the other person's position might be.

1 _____

_____

2 _____

_____

3 _____

_____

4 _____

_____

5 _____

_____

Now write down what is the most important point for you about this issue; what is the thing you most want to gain?

1 _____

_____

2 _____

_____

3 _____

_____

4 _____

_____

5 _____

_____

For each negotiation point list what would you be prepared to give up in order to get what you most want.

1 _____

_____

2 _____

_____

3 _____

_____

4 _____

_____

5 _____

_____

Try to negotiate at least one of these issues in the next few weeks, bearing in mind the points above. Describe here what happened.

_____

_____

_____

_____

_____

Handling difficult moments

There are, of course, endless ways in which our social lives can present us with difficulties. Let's look at three particularly troublesome ones for people who are socially anxious.

1 Criticisms and complaints cause problems for many socially anxious people. This is because they so often fit with your negative self-opinion. If you expect to be judged negatively then receiving a criticism can easily confirm your opinion, and cast you down so far that it is hard to respond.

Is receiving criticism a problem for you? Describe a recent experience here.

_____

_____

_____

_____

_____

2 Most people find **confrontations and conflicts** hard to deal with. This is particularly the case if you're worried about offending or alienating people, or if you feel rejected and cast out when someone is angry with you.

In the space below describe a recent confrontation you found hard to deal with.

_____

_____

_____

_____

_____

3 Finally, **compliments** are often a problem. Compliments are sometimes literally 'incredible', in the sense that they are just seem too far from reality to be believed. However, they can also make you feel so embarrassed that you want to shrink away. Personal remarks of many kinds tend to increase self-consciousness, and may provoke all the dreaded symptoms of social anxiety.

Do compliments make you feel uncomfortable? Describe a recent experience here.

_____

_____

_____

_____

_____

Some of the ways of dealing with these three difficulties are described next.

Criticism and complaints

The key to dealing with complaints and criticisms is to be able to admit to any weaknesses you have **accurately**. This means you neither exaggerate their importance or dismiss them as irrelevant. Of course, when feelings run high this is not easy. And when the expression of those feelings has been stifled the underlying resentment and anger may make it even harder. The skills of cognitive therapy are helpful here.

For example, if someone showed you they were pleased about something you had done, rather than displeased with you, and said: 'Thank you for being so helpful. That was really thoughtful of you,' would you generalize, and react as if this were a definitive judgement on your character? Would you think, 'How true; I'm always a very thoughtful person'?

When being criticized (such as someone saying, 'That was really thoughtless. How could you be so insensitive?') or when a complaint hits home and leaves you feeling rejected ('You're so messy – careless – forgetful – inefficient'), many people, and socially anxious ones in particular, treat the comment as if it were a profound statement of truth. They react as if the criticism reflected a considered judgement about them, rather than a reaction to a particular thing they had done.

But at times, everyone does things wrong, or insensitive things, or things that give offence or that others think are rude. This no more makes them a villain than doing the opposite – being helpful or considerate or friendly – makes them a saint. The mistake is to judge yourself, your whole character, on the basis of one, or a few, actions – whether for good or for bad.

When you are on the receiving end of criticisms and complaints it helps to do the following things:

- Refuse to be labelled (as in thinking, this criticism proves I'm a bad person)

- Accept what is true about the criticism

- Apologize appropriately.

It is enormously helpful to be fair to yourself when you do apologize. Imagine what an impartial judge would say – not what the internal critic and socially anxious voice inside you wants to say. When you apologize, saying 'I'm sorry I upset you. I didn't mean to' is often enough.

When you want to criticize or complain

When you are in the opposite position, and yourself want to make a complaint or criticism, then there are three pointers to bear in mind.

1 **Be clear about what you want to say.** Say what you have to say briefly, without elaboration. This means sticking to the facts and not making guesses about the other person's feelings, or attitudes, or opinions. 'Your car was parked in front of my driveway again today.' 'I have been doing all the chores for both of us this week.'

2 **State your own feelings or opinions.** Be honest about what is bothering you without hot-headed displays of emotion: 'I needed to get my car out, and yours was in the way.' 'I feel taken for granted.'

3 **Specify what you want.** Ask for specific change. Ask for only one thing at a time. 'Please will you park somewhere else?' 'I would like some help clearing up, now.'

These 'rules' may sound unrealistically simple at first sight. However, obeying them is useful. It takes people immediately out of conflict, during which feelings run high and are hard to control. Instead you move into negotiation, which is based on principles of fairness, instead. Practise writing here three complaints or criticisms you would like to make at home or at work, following the 'rules'.

1 _____

_____

_____

_____

_____

2 _____

_____

_____

_____

_____

3 _____

_____

_____

_____

_____

Confrontation and conflict

When confrontation and conflict cannot be avoided it is important to know how to deal with them. When feelings are running high it is hard to think straight. It is much easier to react first and to deal with the consequences – which often involve licking one's wounds – later. The following suggestions are not easy to follow, but will be useful if you can remember them. They are worth learning by heart and practising. If they can become second nature to you, you will avoid a great deal of distress. The main principles are these:

1 Clarify what has upset you, and what is bothering the other person. Ask, and tell. For example, 'I'm angry that you left me out.'

2 Instead of assuming you are right and the other person is wrong, try to think in terms of different points of view. This helps even if one person is wrong.

3 Watch out for escalation: in feelings, in threats, and in the way they are expressed. Often when people are angry on the surface, they are also fearful or hurt under-neath, and paying attention to these feelings may solve the problem.

Some rules of fair fighting

- Keep to the point. Fight on one front at once, without bringing in ancient history.

- Cut out extremist words: 'You *always* ignore what I say.' 'You *never* pull your weight.'

- Take a break to calm down. Do not storm out, but explain what you are doing.

- Think about the part you play in the conflict, and own your own feelings: 'I'm angry about ...', not 'You make me furious'.

- Do not hit where it hurts most. It makes it harder to forgive and forget.

- Blaming and threatening people leads to escalation, not to resolution.

Compliments

Compliments can create difficulties by causing embarrassment. Although you may blush with pleasure when complimented or admired, you may also blush with embarrassment, and wish that you could hide yourself away. It is as if you were fac-ing a threat rather than a compliment.

Why should a compliment make someone feel threatened? One reason is that it makes you the focus of attention, and attention has often been associated with threat in the past – even if this time the attention is favourable rather than unfavourable. Another is that responding to compliments involves using conventions, as if there were a 'formula' to apply. There sometimes seems to be a right way and a wrong way to respond to them. Being covered with confusion may happen partly because it is hard to think what to say.

Dismissing compliments is something for which socially anxious people may well have an overdeveloped skill. You may say things like:

- 'This old thing? I picked it up in a market years ago'

- 'I only did what it said in the cookbook'

- 'I had lots of help. It didn't have much to do with me, really.'

People will do anything to turn the attention elsewhere.

You may fear being conceited or self-satisfied if you accept the compliment. You might believe that if you think too much of yourself, this could be another way in which other people could evaluate you negatively.

It is undoubtedly hard for some people to accept that the compliments they receive are genuine, and not just flattery, or motivated by wanting something from them. It is also hard to accept them gracefully. One way to learn is (genuinely) to give compliments to others, and to learn from their responses what to say yourself. Think about which ways feel right, and try them out. Do not dismiss compliments, or laugh them off, but try to accept them as you might accept another kind of appreciative offering. Ask yourself whether it would make a difference to believe in the compliment.

Make a list here of some of the compliments you could offer to people you know.

_____

_____

_____

_____

_____

Striking a balance

Being assertive is about being fair, to yourself as well as to others. So it makes sense to sum up the main points made in this section by thinking about the numerous kinds of 'balancing acts' that are involved in overcoming social anxiety. Some of these are listed in the box on page 67 and you may like to add your own items to this list.

The point is not to become a fence-sitter, going for neither one thing nor the other, or to become a wishy-washy person with no strong opinions. Instead it's about finding a way of being yourself that involves neither controlling others nor being controlled by them – both of which are extremist positions.

The danger of taking up extremist positions of these kinds it that one extreme seems to alternate with the other. This makes the business of finding the 'happy medium' even harder than usual. Extremist positions go with:

- All-or-nothing thinking (either everything I do is useless, or it's all just fine)

- Black-and-white thinking (If people don't love you, then they hate you)

- Alternating between highs and lows (feeling wonderful about yourself when in a loving relationship, but desperately miserable, or incapable, or rejected when on your own).

The secret to feeling confident, calmer and happier most of the time is in finding more balanced ways of thinking and behaving.

Balancing acts: assertive behaviour avoids extremist positions

- Balancing being interested with being too curious (or nosy)

- Balancing a focus inwards, on your inner experience, with focusing outwards, only on other people

- Balancing talking with listening

- Balancing seeking information on the one hand with disclosing information on the other

- Balancing talking only about feelings with talking mainly about facts

- Balancing recognizing the effects of the past on yourself without being dominated or restricted by it

- Balancing keeping yourself safe at one extreme with barging in where angels fear to tread on the other

- Balancing revealing intimate things about yourself with clamming up, and saying nothing that might give you away, or give people a hold over you

- Finding the halfway house between being passive and being aggressive.

Summary

1 Assertiveness means behaving as if your needs, feelings and emotions are equally important to those of other people.

2 Passive behaviour involves going along with others at your own personal cost.

3 Aggressive behaviour disregards the thoughts, feelings and needs of others.

4 It is important to recognize that you can only change yourself, not others.

5 You can learn how to say 'no' by clarifying your priorities, saying 'no' with assurance and giving yourself time to think.

6 Learning negotiation skills can help you get your needs met in a non-confrontational way.

7 Handle criticism by learning to admit weaknesses accurately without exaggerating them or dismissing them.

8 Try giving compliments in order to learn more about how to receive them.

9 Finding a balance is the key.

SECTION 5: The Legacy of Being Bullied

This section will help you understand:

- What bullying is

- The effects of having been bullied

- How people react to being bullied

- Why someone becomes a bully

- How to overcome the long-term effects of bullying.

Many socially anxious people have sad and distressing stories to tell about periods in their life when they were bullied. They still remember with acute distress what it felt like at the time. Being the subject of bullying can have long-lasting effects and these are especially difficult for socially anxious people to deal with. This section will provide some ideas about how to overcome these long-term effects.

Some facts about bullying

Many people describe bullying as 'primitive', or instinctive behaviour. This is because bullies seem to have a basic need to hide their own vulnerability by controlling other people. Their thinking goes like this: If I am top dog then I will be able to get my own way, and other people are less likely to attack me. This will be even more likely for bullies who gather a group of followers around them.

Bullying can be found in all walks of life. It happens to adults as well as to children, at home, at school and at work, and it happens throughout the world. What is more, it is probably true to say that everyone has done it sometimes – to a degree. But mature people, supposedly, hardly ever do it. They do not need to, partly because they have learned how to negotiate, or to collaborate, or to live and to let live. They have no need to protect or support themselves by gaining control over others.

Being fair – to yourself as well as to others – is the opposite of bullying. Assertive behaviour, which we looked at in Section 4, makes bullying unnecessary and being bullied irrelevant.

But assertiveness skills alone may not be enough. This is especially the case when organizations such as schools, clubs or workplaces ignore or encourage bullying behaviour. When it is hard, or even impossible, for one person to stand up against the group, then the culture or social context within which bullying occurs needs to change.

Bullying can be both obvious and subtle. It can range from relatively harmless and more or less affectionate kinds of teasing through to intimidation or victimization. Using threats and taunts are some of the most obvious bullying behaviours. The more subtle ones may be harder to recognize at first. They include:

- Picking on people, or in some way singling them out for 'special' treatment
- Seeking out personal information and then disclosing it to others, or betraying a trust
- Excluding people, especially from positions of leadership, or isolating them
- Making general rather than specific criticisms and accusations that appear to apply to the whole person rather than to something that they did or said
- Sabotaging someone's plans or activities
- Making unreasonable demands
- Using gossip, innuendo or manipulation
- And many others.

Clearly, bullying is not just one thing: it involves many different kinds of language and behaviour. What makes any of these bullying behaviour is the intention to control or exclude people. The result is they feel they no longer belong to the group to which the bully does belong. Bullying works by making use of intimidation and humiliation.

Have you been bullied at home, school or later in life? Describe your experience here. Who bullied you?

What did they do?

_____

_____

_____

_____

_____

How did that make you feel?

_____

_____

_____

_____

_____

How did the bullying end?

_____

_____

_____

_____

_____

Some effects of being bullied

Bullying exists in all degrees, from the relatively trivial to the horrendous. Being seriously bullied can be enormously stressful. It affects every aspect of life:

- Your feelings or emotions
- Your body
- All the levels of thinking that were described in Part One, Section 5
- The way you behave.

For example, being bullied is frightening, but it can also make people feel angry, resentful and frustrated. When it seems that there is nothing to be done about it and no way out, people can feel hopeless and depressed as well. It makes people physically tense, on edge, unable to relax or to sleep, and likely to suffer visible symptoms of distress such as trembling or sweating.

Your waking life may be dominated by a sense of dread. You may constantly keep on the look out for 'dangerous' situations and think about what might happen next. You may also be haunted by memories or images of recent distressing experiences. Disturbing dreams may prevent you sleeping at night. Your daily behaviour will be a product of all these experiences, and this in turn will seriously interfere with your ability to do the things you wish to do, in the ways that you otherwise would.

However, the end result of being bullied varies greatly. For some people it appears to have no lasting effects, but for others it does more damage, and leaves an apparently permanent scar. Of course, the worse the bullying the worse the effects are likely to be, and the longer they are likely to last. But another factor is also important, and that is the meaning of the bullying to the person who was on the receiving end of it.

The meaning of the message

The messages that people take away with them when they were bullied can play an important part in what happens next. For example, imagine you were tormented at school for being unable to pronounce your 'r's' properly. You might see this as saying more about other people than yourself. You might think how silly they were to pick on something so unimportant when making judgements about you. It might then have no lasting effect on your self-opinion.

On the other hand you might see this as an attack on yourself; as having identified a very real personal failing. In that case it could leave you with a deep-seated uncertainty about yourself and your acceptability, and with your confidence shaken.

The personal meaning to you of what happened helps to determine the precise form of the beliefs and assumptions that continue to influence you later on. It is in this way that the experience of bullying can link up with the features of social anxiety. Read through the statements below and place a tick beside those you feel apply to you. You may well find some statements are very similar to the symptoms of social anxiety you've already identified in Part One.

Beliefs

- [ ] I'm not acceptable as I am
- [ ] I don't belong
- [ ] People will reject me
- [ ] Nobody can be trusted

Assumptions

- [ ] I've got to get people's approval, or they will exclude me
- [ ] The only way not to be bullied is to hit before you get hit
- [ ] If you let people get to know you they will take advantage of you
- [ ] It's best not to tangle with powerful people, or with anyone in a position of authority

Level of attention

- [ ] I notice people's frowns, or signs of criticism, or judgements
- [ ] I'm always checking out how I'm coming over to other people

Behaviours, including safety behaviours and avoidance

- [ ] I try to protect myself to hide my 'weaknesses'; I become secretive
- [ ] I try to please people, and to gain their approval; I try to do things 'right'
- [ ] I keep myself to myself; I don't join in, or get socially involved
- [ ] I accommodate to what I think others expect, for instance by hiding my anger

Self-consciousness and self-awareness

- [ ] I think about how I look, or speak, or behave
- [ ] I make sure that I never say or do anything that might offend people
- [ ] Embarrassment comes easily, for example when I'm talking about personal feelings or needs

The things that socially anxious people, and some shy people, tend to believe about themselves and about others clearly have something in common with the messages that being bullied can provide. Social anxiety focuses on the fear of being evaluated or judged: on the fear of doing something that will be humiliating or embarrassing. Bullies do just that: they evaluate and judge their victims and openly humiliate and embarrass them. It is hardly surprising that bullying can sometimes make social anxiety worse, and make it difficult to fight against it.

Reactions to being bullied

Many people blame themselves for being bullied. It's as if they have taken on the criticisms, accusations or taunts that they received and come to believe that they were true.

Of course, there may have been an element of truth in these taunts. Children may get picked on for being too short or too tall or for some other characteristic for which they cannot be held responsible. But the fact that you may have been shorter than most other people in your class does not justify the bullying behaviour. It is the bully and not the victim who is to blame. If you were in a school, club or workplace that failed to prevent the bullying happening, then that organization is to blame too. So, if you were bullied, that was not your fault.

Nor is it your fault if you could not find a way of stopping it. Many ways of responding to a bully have been found to make the problem worse, not better, at least on some occasions. If you tried them and failed, this does not mean that you were weak, or stupid, or not courageous enough. You might like to tick any of the approaches below that you tried:

☐ Explaining yourself, or justifying your behaviour

☐ Seeking to gain approval, and to please the people who hurt you

☐ Defending yourself or standing up for yourself

☐ Giving as good as you got, or fighting back

☐ Trying to let it ride over you; ignoring it and doing nothing about it.

If people told you not to let it happen, or to show that you could give as good as you got, or if they left you with the impression that you asked for it, or laid yourself open to it, or deserved it in some way, then they too were wrong. Once again, the person who 'got it wrong' was the bully – not the target.

Understanding the bully

At this point it's helpful to try to understand what motivates a child who bullies. Bullies often feel extremely vulnerable themselves, and may not be well supported by the people around them. Their primitive need for acceptance and approval is often – though not necessarily – based on a strong sense of their own inadequacy or isolation.

Bullies may feel inferior and vulnerable too, and can only deal with these feelings in quite simplistic ways. They often pick on people who threaten them in some way, for example by being more clever, or more competent, or more acceptable. This is why it is so important that schools develop clear policies for dealing with the problem. Schools need to make it possible for both bullies and bullied to develop more mature ways of reacting to the challenges that confront them. They need to ensure that both the victim and the aggressor receive more of the help and support that they need.

Think about someone who bullied you or was a well-known bully at school. Do you know anything about their personal life that might explain their behaviour?

_____

_____

_____

_____

_____

Overcoming the more enduring effects of being bullied

The main message here is: 'It's OK to be you.' As we saw in Part One, Section 1, page 3, people who are shy and socially anxious have as many of the characteristics that people value and admire as everyone else. There is no need to keep these characteristics hidden – from yourself or from others. Learning how to express them, and to develop them, helps to make you more spontaneous and less inhibited or self-conscious in your interactions with others. This in turn develops the sense that you can trust yourself when you are with other people. You will feel assured that they are not trying to manipulate or control you.

All of the methods described in Part Two of this self-help course can be used to help overcome the after-effects of being bullied. You can combine them with the skills described in Section 4 of Part Three for making your voice heard in assertive ways. The following points are intended as reminders. They can help you to work out what to do if you feel that being bullied earlier in life has left you with a legacy that you would now like to leave behind.

Identify your internal critical voice

Do you have favourite ways of putting yourself down? Do you say to yourself, 'I'm no good' or 'Idiot'? A bad habit learned from bullies is to go to extremes when making judgements about yourself, and even to echo judgements that you have heard earlier. List here some of the ways in which you put yourself down that echo things bullies have said to you in the past.

_____

_____

_____

_____

Think about the message your bully's words and actions left you with. Try to free yourself from the old judgement and its painful implications by recognizing it for what it is: a primitive reaction made for primitive reasons that had nothing to do with your value or worth or acceptability as a person even then – let alone now.

Answer the bully back now, and write down some more positive and realistic judgements about yourself. If you get stuck look at what you wrote on page 3 of Part One and on page 71 of Part Two, when you thought about your strengths and your social successes.

_____

_____

_____

_____

_____

_____

When you do something that bothers you, then it is the behaviour that you should evaluate, and not yourself as a person. Watch out for any tendency to label yourself and take care not to over-generalize (see Part Two, Section 3, page 56), or you will be giving too much significance to one aspect of yourself or your behaviour.

Identify your triggers

All sorts of things may remind you of some of the bad things that have happened to you earlier in life. These could include:

- The actions of others
- Being spoken to in a certain tone of voice
- A physical similarity with someone who bullied you
- Being around powerful or controlling people, or people who have authority over you
- All sorts of sights, sounds and smells.

Memories and images can be easily triggered, and they often bring strong feelings with them. They may also seem to come automatically, but are so fleeting that you may recognize a familiar feeling – of dread, or inferiority, or vulnerability of some kind – without being aware of what provoked it.

For example, if you were cold-shouldered, excluded or ignored as a child, then similar feelings might be provoked in **any** situation in which you are not heard. This could include trying to catch the attention of a busy salesperson or the waiter in a restaurant.

List here some of your triggers that remind you of when you were bullied. If you can identify your trigger it may help you cope better with powerful emotions when they arise.

_____

_____

_____

_____

_____

_____

Think about how your reactions may maintain problems now

Imagine that you learned the hard way that it was dangerous to let people know too much about you. So you developed ways of not letting your reactions show, and learnt to keep a deadpan expression on your face. At the time of being bullied this could well have been a sensible and effective reaction that prevented some of the attacks that might otherwise have come your way.

But this reserve can become a habit, and can easily be misinterpreted later on. It is surprising how many people with warm hearts and sensitive reactions come over as distant and cold when they feel nervous in company. It can be very hard to acknowledge and to recognize this is the impression you give people when it's exactly the opposite to the way you feel.

Reserve and distance is built on an old and out of date assumption: 'If I let people see my reactions I will be making myself vulnerable to attack'. But this assumption leads to behaviour that gives the wrong impression to others. Your behaviour misleads people about what you are really like. Although it can feel risky at first, showing your sensitivity and responsiveness helps people to warm to you. They will come to realize that the initial appearance of you being cold or distant was wrong.

Think about ways you behave in order to keep yourself safe from bullying. What do you do? And does this way of behaving help or hinder you?

_____

_____

_____

_____

_____

_____

_____

The general point here is that your original reactions to being bullied, while they were probably helpful at the time, may subsequently keep the problem going. Think about how you originally reacted. Think about what you learned to do to protect yourself, or to keep yourself safe, and try to put these old reactions on hold for a while. See if doing so makes it easier to be yourself and to be happy with that. You might find it helpful to re-read the section on safety behaviours in Part Two, Section 4.

Re-examine your beliefs about your value or worth

Bullies often make people feel worthless: as if they had no value. If this is what you believe about yourself then your beliefs need updating. It is no wonder that this is the message that you took away at the time. It is hard not to believe the things that other people say about you when you are young and when these things are repeated and backed up by bullying tactics. The most important thing to remember is that your worth is never determined by what others think of you, good or bad. This is especially the case if your evidence for such an undermining self-opinion comes from the opinion of someone who bullied you.

If your beliefs are a problem, re-read the section on underlying beliefs and assumptions, pp 11–40.

Develop a system of support

People who have been cast down by others need subsequently to be affirmed instead. In the end, it is being aware of your own strengths and positive characteristics, your talents and skills and preferences and interests, that provides a solid basis for self-affirmation. No one else can do it for you entirely, but having a network of supporters undoubtedly helps. Knowing that there are people who see your point of view reduces the sense of being alone and isolated. Letting them know how you think and feel about things, and being prepared to make your needs known, is one way of developing a sense of shared ideas and attitudes, and even of shared experiences during childhood.

Review the list of friends and supporters you made on page 44 and think about who among them might particularly help you feel more supported and affirmed. Write down their names here.

_____

_____

_____

_____

_____

_____

_____

Some final points to bear in mind

Section 4 emphasized the importance of striking a balance when it comes to being assertive. The same approach is useful when you're overcoming the after-effects of bullying. Strike a balance between:

- Pleasing other people and pleasing yourself

- Seeking approval and ignoring what others think

- Going your own way and accommodating what others want.

In order to find out what suits you, and to develop the confidence to be yourself in the way that feels right, use the mini-experiments we described in Part Two, Section 4, pp. 85–103. Then you can try things out and think carefully about what happens when you do. As we said at the beginning of this section, being yourself is fine. You just need to find out what makes you feel more confident and more comfortable about being the way that you are.

Summary

1   Being bullied can have lasting effects, and these may be particularly hard for people who are socially anxious or shy to overcome.

2   If you were bullied, that does not mean that it was your fault. Nor does it mean that you were too weak or inept to stop it happening. Bullying is 'primitive' behaviour that is most effectively controlled by people leading the group in which it occurs.

3   In order to get over the effects of having been bullied it is helpful to:
   - identify your critical voice
   - identify the triggers that remind you of what happened
   - think about how your reactions might work to maintain problems now
   - re-examine your beliefs about your value and self-worth
   - develop a system that provides you with support.

4   Use some mini-experiments to help you to strike a balance between being controlled by others and protecting yourself by keeping yourself separate from them.

SECTION 6: Relaxation

Anxiety and worry make you tense, and tension has a host of painful effects. It leads to physical aches and pains; it can make you tired and irritable; it can drag you down or wind you up; and it eats up energy fast. It is easy to recognize that it would help to be able to relax better, but it is not easy to do. There are now a great many books, videotapes and cassette tapes on relaxation available in the shops, and many health or leisure centres have information about local classes, so you may be able to find a method that you like quite easily. If not, the brief instructions on progressive muscular relaxation provided here provide a good starting point for teaching yourself how to relax.

Relaxation has to be learned

Life would be much easier if relaxation came naturally, but for many people it does not, and then it is necessary to make a conscious effort to learn how to do it. Relaxation is a skill, which means that if you are going to become good at it you will have to learn what to do and then practise doing it. One of the problems is that learning how to relax is not one thing, but many. It is:

- An attitude: taking things more in your stride, and more calmly

- A physical skill: learning how to recognize and release physical tension

- A habit: developing routines that wind you down rather than wind you up

- Restorative: a way of giving yourself rest and recreation, that can be interesting, or stimulating, or pleasurable, as well as relaxing

There is plenty of research showing that people find relaxation helpful, but little comparing the different methods. Therefore it seems reasonable to choose whichever method attracts you and to stick with it. Whichever method you use, it is helpful to think of yourself as learning how to relax in four stages. First you need to prepare yourself, so that you can focus on what you are doing without being distracted; second, you need to practise relaxing, so that you know what you are trying to do; third, you need consciously to apply what you have learned, so that you can use it to help yourself; and fourth, you should think of extending what you have learned in ways that help you to adopt a relaxed lifestyle. Going through these four stages will help you to take advantage of all the different aspects of relaxation, and one way of doing it, using progressive muscular relaxation, is described below.

Stage 1: Preparation

Find yourself time, and find yourself a comfortable place in which to practise. You will need at least half an hour a day at first, and if you are a busy person – or a disorganized one – it may be hard to set yourself a regular routine and to stick to it. You should make sure that you will not be disturbed while you are practising (even unplugging the telephone before you begin), and your comfortable place needs to support your body well, and to be warm. Many of the relaxation methods can be learned either sitting or lying down, but if you do them in bed, late at night, you may find that you fall asleep while you are doing them. Although you may want to use the method later on to help you to sleep better, it is more sensible at first to practise relaxing when you are not likely to fall asleep so that you can concentrate on the things you are supposed to be learning: how to recognize the many differences between being tense and being relaxed, how to pick up your own signs of tension and trouble spots, and – most important of all – how to let them go when you feel you need to.

Having made yourself comfortable, start by focusing on your breathing, and trying to breathe in a relaxed and calm way. Relaxed breathing is slow and regular, and when you are deeply relaxed your stomach will rise and fall as you breathe in and out. Tense breathing is relatively rapid and shallow, and it makes your chest move up and down, sometimes quite rapidly. One way to learn about your breathing is to place one hand on your chest and one on your stomach and to see which moves most. If you do this at a time when you are really relaxed you will find that the hand on your chest hardly moves at all. If you are breathing in a tense way then just try to slow yourself down gently, by degrees. You could pace yourself by counting slowly as you breathe out, saying, for example, 'one thousand, two thousand, three thousand ...'. Try to ensure that you have completely emptied your lungs before you inhale again. It may also help to say something to yourself, like 'let go', as you breathe out, to start yourself thinking about being more relaxed.

When you are learning to relax, go at your own pace. There is no hurry, and becoming impatient or self-conscious about it can be counter-productive.

Stage 2: Practice

Learn to relax your body by first tensing up and then letting go groups of muscles, one by one. This works well because it is hard, when you are tense, to obey the instruction 'relax', but it is relatively easy to focus on one part of your body at a time and to tighten up those muscles even if they are already somewhat tense. Doing so, for example by clenching your fists, makes you immediately aware of the tension in those muscles. When they start to ache or to hurt then it is easy to let them go, and tensing up first helps them to relax more fully than they otherwise might. When you relax after tensing your muscles up you may even feel the blood flow back again, making you feel warmer as you become more deeply relaxed. If you breathe out as you let the muscles go you will be using the body's natural rhythms to help you to relax.

The basic exercise is simple. Tense up a particular group of muscles. Hold the tension for a short while. Then let the tension go. If you can breathe out when you let go, you will find that it helps in letting the tension subside even further. Give yourself time for all the tension to drain away before you move on to tighten up the next part of your body. You could tell yourself to relax, or to let go, as you exhale for the next few breaths, so that you make a conscious association between giving yourself this message and the feeling of being more relaxed. You could also imagine your body becoming increasingly heavy, or limp, or floppy as the tension in it dies away.

Focus on each part of your body in turn, repeating the same basic exercise. As you progress, try to concentrate fully on each part of the body, and to tense the next bit up without losing too much of the relaxation that you have already achieved. Usually people learn to relax their hands and arms first, then work up from their feet to their head, in the order shown on page 84.

Do not leap up quickly after doing your relaxation exercises, or you might feel dizzy; give yourself time to start up gradually.

Stage 3: Application

No one can remain deeply relaxed while carrying out normal daily activities, nor while feeling anxious or worried, so the next step is to learn how to apply what you have learned in ways that will be more useful. If you can recognize small degrees of tension early, before they have built up, it will be easier to relax your way out of them. To do this you need to shorten the exercises and to practise relaxing in increasingly difficult situations.

Progressive muscular relaxation

Work through the parts of the body in a regular order so as not to forget any of the muscle groups. Focus your attention on each part of the body as you tense it up, then give yourself as much time as you need to let the tension go. As you learn how to relax you may notice small degrees of tension more easily. If you find it difficult to release tension in one place, such as your neck, or back, you may need a double dose of the basic exercise for that part of your body.

Hands: Clench the fists.

Arms: Tighten up your biceps and lower arms, e.g. by pushing them down.

Shoulders: Raise your shoulders as if they could touch your ears.

Feet: Screw up your toes.

Front of legs: Point your toes as you stretch your legs out.

Back of legs: Flex your feet up and push your heels away from you.

Thighs: Tighten them as you press your knees down.

Bottom: Clench your buttocks together.

Stomach: Hold your stomach muscles in tight.

Lower back: Press the small of your back into the chair or floor.

Chest: Breathe in, hold your breath, and tighten your chest muscles.

Shoulders: Raise your shoulders as if to touch your ears. Breathe in as you tighten up.

Neck: (1) Stretch your head up, as if your chin could touch the ceiling.
       (2) Bend your head forward until your chin reaches your chest.

Mouth and jaw: Press your lips together and clench your teeth.

Eyes: Close them up tight.

Forehead and scalp: Raise your eyebrows as if they could disappear into your hair.

Face: Screw all the muscles up together.

There are many ways of shortening relaxation exercises, for example working on the body in bigger chunks (arms, legs, body and face); working through the first few exercises and then focusing on the other parts of your body to see if you can become aware of the remaining tension and let it go; or leaving out the tension and working only on the relaxation. Shortened exercises are usually more helpful if they include an instruction to yourself, like 'keep calm', and you start by trying to breathe in a relaxed way. The more practice you give yourself, the quicker this stage will go. So once you can relax more quickly in peace and quiet, start trying to apply the method in other situations also. Remind yourself often as you go through the day to check your level of tension. Then you could take a deep breath in, hold it for a moment and as you let it go drop your shoulders and tell yourself to relax. Or you could set your watch to bleep every so often and do one small 'tense and relax' exercise every time you hear it. The shorter your exercise, the more often you should practise.

If you find it easier to relax physically than mentally, then you may also find it useful to consciously bring relaxing images into your mind as you practise relaxing. The images you choose should be those that have strong associations for you with being relaxed. The sorts of things that other people choose include being in a quiet, peaceful part of the country; looking into a picture of something beautiful, watching the sea or the sky when the weather is calm, or being somewhere warm and comfortable where – at least temporarily – no demands will be made upon you. Try consciously to turn your mind, when it wanders to your fears or worries, to one of these images instead, and make use of all your senses in the imagery, so that you might become aware of what you could hear, feel and smell in your image, as well as what you could see.

Do not be surprised if your images change, and your mind wanders away from them, as images constantly change. However, if your mind wanders back to the things that make you feel tense then try to re-establish the more relaxing imagery, and start again from there.

It is always easier to relax when you can start by making yourself comfortable in a quiet and warm place. Once you are reasonably sure that you know how to do it, try doing brief relaxation exercises when you are sitting at a table, or walking somewhere, or eating a meal. Practise relaxing while carrying out everyday activities first, and then move on to relaxing when doing something more difficult for you, like talking on the telephone. You will certainly not be able to apply your relaxation skills in situations that make you extremely anxious at first, but the more practice you have the more you will improve – and you can certainly use them to help you calm down after being in a tight spot. Develop your skills by applying them as often as you can, especially if you are taken by surprise by a situation that troubles you.

Stage 4: Extension

Being relaxed is an attitude as well as the result of learning a practical skill. Here are some ways to develop a more relaxed attitude.

Adopt a relaxed posture. Do you find yourself sitting on the edge of your chair? Or fidgeting and fiddling with things? Or hurrying about with your head tucked into your shoulders and your eyes on the ground? Tension wastes energy, so allow your body to rest whenever you can.

Stop rushing about. This is an exhausting habit, and quickly wears you out. Most people get just as much done when they do it more slowly and calmly, and they can also keep going for longer, at a more relaxed pace.

Plan to do some things that you find relaxing. It does not matter whether these things are strenuous (like gardening, or going for a run), or more peaceful (like listening to music or watching TV). It is the fact that they help you to relax that is helpful.

Seek out things that you enjoy, and that give you pleasure. The more you are enjoying yourself, the more relaxed you will feel.

Spread the risks. If you put all your eggs in one basket, a threat to that basket will make you extremely tense.

Give yourself breaks. Take short breaks, like half an hour looking at a magazine, as well as longer ones, like a day out or a holiday.

Useful Information

Useful organizations and online services

Great Britain

British Association of Behavioural and Cognitive Psychotherapies (BABCP)
The Globe Centre
PO Box 9
Accrington BB5 0XB
Tel: 01254 875 277
Email: babcp@babcp.com
Website: www.babcp.org.uk

British Association for Counselling and Psychotherapy (BACP)
BACP House
15 St John's Business Park
Lutterworth
Leicestershire LE17 4HB
Tel: 0870 443 5252
Email: bacp@bacp.co.uk
Website: www.bacp.co.uk

FearFighter
Website: www.fearfighter.com

(This website helps sufferers to identify specific problems and develop and work on treatment of those problems)

MIND: The National Association for Mental Health
Granta House
15-19 Broadway
Stratford
London E15 4BQ
MindinfoLine: 0845 766 0163

(Can also give you details of local tranquillizer withdrawal support groups)
Email: contact@mind.org.uk

National Phobics Society
Zion Community Resource Centre
339 Stretford Road
Hulme
Manchester M15 4ZY
Tel: 0870 122 2325
Fax: 0161 226 7727
Email: info@phobics-society.org.uk
Website: www.phobics-society.org.uk

No Panic
93 Brands Farm
Randlay
Telford TF3 2JQ
Helpline: 0808 808 0545 (10 a.m.–10 p.m.)
Email: ceo@nopanic.org.uk
Website: www.nopanic.org.uk

Social Anxiety UK
Email: contact@social-anxiety.org.uk
Website: www.social-anxiety.org.uk

Australia

Anxiety Disorders Association, Victoria (ADAVIC)
PO Box 625
Kew
VIC 3101
Tel: 0061 03 9853 8089
Email: adavic@adavic.org.au
Website: home.vicnet.net.au/~adavic/

Anxiety Recovery Centre, Victoria
PO Box 358
Mt Waverley
VIC 3149
OCD and Anxiety Helpline: 0061 03 9886 9377
Email: arcmail@arcvic.com.au
Website: www.arcvic.com.au

Mental Health Association (Qld), Inc.
Fleming House
Orford Drive
WACOL
Qld 4076
Tel/Fax: 0061 07 3271 5544
Website: www.mentalhealth.org.au

Mood Gym
Website: www.moodgym.anu.edu.au

(An online service offering information on cognitive behavioral therapy provided by the Australian National University)

Social Anxiety Australia (SAA)
PO Box 94
Indooroopilly
Queensland
Australia 4068
Tel: 0061 07 3366 7726
Email: contact@socialanxiety.com.au
Website: www.socialanxietyaustralia.com.au

New Zealand

Everybody
Website: www.everybody.co.nz

(This website provides useful and accurate health information written by medical writers and reviewed by consumer health organizations and health professionals)

Social Anxiety Support Group
Floor 2
Securities House
221 Gloucester Street
PO Box 13167
Christchurch
Tel: 0064 03 377 9665
Fax: 0064 03 365 5345
Website: www.socialphobia.org.nz

USA

American Mental Health Foundation
2 East 86th Street
New York NY 1008

(Written enquiries only)

Anxiety Disorders Association of America (ADAA)
Tel: 001 240 485 1001
Fax: 001 240 485 1035
Website: www.adaa.org

The Association for Behavioral and Cognitive Therapies (ABCT)
(Formerly the Association for the Advancement of Behavior Therapy)
305 7th Avenue
16th Floor
New York NY 10001
Tel: 001 212 647 1890
Fax: 001 212 647 1865
Website: www.aabt.org

Drinker's Check-up
Website: www.drinkerscheckup.com

(A website designed to help you understand your drinking patterns and how to change them.)

Institute for Behavior Therapy
104 East 40th Street
Suite 206
New York NY 10016
Tel: 001 212 692 9288
Fax: 001 212 692 9305

MentalHelp.net
Website: www.mentalhelp.net/psyhelp

(MentalHelp.net provides advice from health professionals, reviews on the latest books on mental health issues and further contact details for related organizations.)

Social Phobia/Social Anxiety Association (SP/SAA)
2058 E. Topeka Drive
Phoenix AZ 85024
Website: www.socialphobia.org

Social Anxiety Institute (SAI)
Website: www.socialanxietyinstitute.org

Useful books

There are many good self-help books covering an enormous range of issues from varying perspectives. Different books appeal to different people and the best way to find the right books for you might be to browse through your local bookshop, or to get recommendations from friends you trust. Some good books that others have found useful are listed.

In this series, in addition to this self-help course, you may find the following books useful:

Michael Crowe, *Overcoming Relationship Problems*, London, Robinson, 2005

Colin A. Espie, *Overcoming Insomnia and Sleep Problems*, London, Robinson, 2006

Melanie Fennell, *Overcoming Low Self-esteem*, London, Robinson, 1999

Paul Gilbert, *Overcoming Depression* (revised edition), London, Robinson, 2000

Helen Kennerley, *Overcoming Anxiety*, London, Robinson, 1997

Some other books on social anxiety:

Debra Hope, Richard G. Heimberg and Cynthia L. Turk, *Managing Social Anxiety*, New York, Oxford University Press Inc., 2006

Ronald M. Rapee, *Overcoming Shyness and Social Phobia*, New York, Jason Aronson, 1998

Sue Spence, Ronald M. Rapee and Vanessa Cobham, *Helping Your Anxious Child*, Oakland, New Harbinger Publications, 2000

A selection of books on related subjects that are generally helpful:

Edmund J. Bourne, *The Anxiety and Phobia Workbook* (fourth edition), Oakland, New Harbinger Publications 2005

Martha Davis, Elizabeth Robbins Eshelman and Matthew McKay, *The Relaxation and Stress Reduction Workbook* (fifth edition), Oakland, New Harbinger Publications, 2000

Windy Dryden, *Overcoming Jealousy*, London, Sheldon Press, 2005

John Gray, *Men are from Mars, Women are from Venus*, London, HarperCollins, 2002

Dennis Greenberger and Christine Padesky, *Mind over Mood*, New York, Guilford Press, 1995

Harriet G. Lerner, *The Dance of Anger*, New York, HarperCollins, 1999

Thich Nhat Hanh, *The Miracle of Mindfulness*, London, Rider, 1991

Matthew McKay, Carole Honeychurch and Patrick Fanning, *The Self-esteem Companion*, Oakland, New Harbinger Publications, 2005

Sue Quilliam, *Stop Arguing Start Talking*, London, Vermilion, 2001

Dorothy Rowe, *Depression* (third edition), Hove, Brunner-Routledge, 2003

Deborah Tannen, *You Just Don't Understand: Women and Men in Conversation*, London, Virago, 1991

Extra Charts and Worksheets

Thought record for challenging beliefs

Situation (be specific)	Upsetting thoughts (keep the different thoughts separate)	Possible alternatives (there may be more than one)	Change in feelings (–10 to +10)	Action plan (what would you like to do differently)

Thought record for challenging beliefs

Situation (be specific)	Upsetting thoughts (keep the different thoughts separate)	Possible alternatives (there may be more than one)	Change in feelings (–10 to +10)	Action plan (what would you like to do differently)

Thought record for challenging beliefs

Situation (be specific)	Upsetting thoughts (keep the different thoughts separate)	Possible alternatives (there may be more than one)	Change in feelings (−10 to +10)	Action plan (what would you like to do differently)

Thought record for challenging beliefs

Situation (be specific)	Upsetting thoughts (keep the different thoughts separate)	Possible alternatives (there may be more than one)	Change in feelings (–10 to +10)	Action plan (what would you like to do differently)

Counter-belief worksheet

Step 1. Belief:

_____

_____

Step 2. How much do you believe this (0–100 per cent)?

_____

THE FORWARD SEARCH PLAN

Before the event

Step 3. Think of a future situation that will be difficult for you

_____

_____

Step 4. Your expectation or prediction (this should fit with your belief)

_____

_____

Step 5. Search plan: What should you be looking out for?

_____

_____

After the event

Step 6. Outcome: What actually happened?

_____

_____

Step 7. What conclusions can you draw from that?

_____

_____

Step 8. Rethinking your original belief

How much do you believe it now (0–100 per cent)?

_____

How would you like to change your belief, now?

_____

_____

Counter-belief worksheet

Step 1. Belief:

_____

_____

Step 2. How much do you believe this (0–100 per cent)?

_____

THE FORWARD SEARCH PLAN

Before the event

Step 3. Think of a future situation that will be difficult for you

_____

_____

Step 4. Your expectation or prediction (this should fit with your belief)

_____

_____

Step 5. Search plan: What should you be looking out for?

_____

_____

After the event

Step 6. Outcome: What actually happened?

_____

_____

Step 7. What conclusions can you draw from that?

_____

_____

Step 8. Rethinking your original belief
How much do you believe it now (0–100 per cent)?

_____

How would you like to change your belief, now?

_____

_____

Counter-belief worksheet

Step 1. Belief:

_____

_____

Step 2. How much do you believe this (0–100 per cent)?

_____

THE FORWARD SEARCH PLAN

Before the event

Step 3. Think of a future situation that will be difficult for you

_____

_____

Step 4. Your expectation or prediction (this should fit with your belief)

_____

_____

Step 5. Search plan: What should you be looking out for?

_____

_____

After the event

Step 6. Outcome: What actually happened?

_____

_____

Step 7. What conclusions can you draw from that?

_____

_____

Step 8. Rethinking your original belief
How much do you believe it now (0–100 per cent)?

_____

How would you like to change your belief, now?

_____

_____

Counter-belief worksheet

Step 1. Belief:

_____

_____

Step 2. How much do you believe this (0–100 per cent)?

_____

THE FORWARD SEARCH PLAN

Before the event

Step 3. Think of a future situation that will be difficult for you

_____

_____

Step 4. Your expectation or prediction (this should fit with your belief)

_____

_____

Step 5. Search plan: What should you be looking out for?

_____

_____

After the event

Step 6. Outcome: What actually happened?

_____

_____

Step 7. What conclusions can you draw from that?

_____

_____

Step 8. Rethinking your original belief

How much do you believe it now (0–100 per cent)?

_____

How would you like to change your belief, now?

_____

_____

Building more positive beliefs

New belief 1:

_____

_____

_____

_____

_____

Information that fits with this new belief:

_____

_____

_____

_____

_____

Draft new belief 2:

_____

_____

_____

_____

_____

Information that fits with this belief:

_____

_____

_____

_____

_____

Building more positive beliefs

New belief 1:

_____

_____

_____

_____

_____

Information that fits with this new belief:

_____

_____

_____

_____

_____

Draft new belief 2:

_____

_____

_____

_____

_____

Information that fits with this belief:

_____

_____

_____

_____

_____

Building more positive beliefs

New belief 1:

_____

_____

_____

_____

Information that fits with this new belief:

_____

_____

_____

_____

Draft new belief 2:

_____

_____

_____

_____

Information that fits with this belief:

_____

_____

_____

_____

Building more positive beliefs

New belief 1:

_____

_____

_____

_____

Information that fits with this new belief:

_____

_____

_____

_____

Draft new belief 2:

_____

_____

_____

_____

Information that fits with this belief:

_____

_____

_____

_____

Challenging your assumptions

Assumption:

_____

_____

Old behaviour:

_____

_____

New behaviour:

_____

_____

Evaluation:

_____

_____

Assumption:

_____

_____

Old behaviour:

_____

_____

New behaviour:

_____

_____

Evaluation:

_____

_____

Assumption:

_____

_____

Old behaviour:

_____

_____

New behaviour:

_____

_____

Evaluation:

_____

_____

Challenging your assumptions

Assumption:

_____

_____

Old behaviour:

_____

New behaviour:

_____

_____

Evaluation:

_____

_____

Assumption:

_____

_____

Old behaviour:

_____

_____

New behaviour:

_____

_____

Evaluation:

_____

_____

Assumption:

_____

_____

Old behaviour:

_____

_____

New behaviour:

_____

_____

Evaluation:

_____

_____

Challenging your assumptions

Assumption:

_____

_____

Old behaviour:

_____

_____

New behaviour:

_____

_____

Evaluation:

_____

_____

Assumption:

_____

_____

Old behaviour:

_____

_____

New behaviour:

_____

_____

Evaluation:

_____

_____

Assumption:

_____

_____

Old behaviour:

_____

_____

New behaviour:

_____

_____

Evaluation:

_____

_____

Challenging your assumptions

Assumption:

_____

_____

Old behaviour:

_____

_____

New behaviour:

_____

_____

Evaluation:

_____

_____

Assumption:

_____

_____

Old behaviour:

_____

_____

New behaviour:

_____

_____

Evaluation:

_____

_____

Assumption:

_____

_____

Old behaviour:

_____

_____

New behaviour:

_____

_____

Evaluation:

_____

_____

Thoughts and Reflections

Thoughts and Reflections

112

Thoughts and Reflections

Thoughts and Reflections

Thoughts and Reflections

Order further books in the Overcoming series

Quantity	Title	Price	Total
	An Introduction to Coping with Anxiety (pack of 10 booklets)	£10.00	
	An Introduction to Coping with Depression (pack of 10 booklets)	£10.00	
	An Introduction to Coping with Health Anxiety (pack of 10 booklets)	£10.00	
	An Introduction to Coping with Panic (pack of 10 booklets)	£10.00	
	An Introduction to Coping with Phobias (pack of 10 booklets)	£10.00	
	An Introduction to Coping with Obsessive Compulsive Disorder (pack of 10 booklets)	£10.00	
	Overcoming Anxiety Self-Help Course	£21.00	
	Overcoming Bulimia Nervosa and Binge-Eating Self-Help Course	£21.00	
	Overcoming Low Self-Esteem Self-Help Course	£21.00	
	Overcoming Panic and Agoraphobia Self-Help Course	£21.00	
	Overcoming Anger and Irritability	£9.99	
	Overcoming Anorexia Nervosa	£9.99	
	Overcoming Anxiety	£9.99	
	Bulimia Nervosa and Binge-Eating	£9.99	
	Overcoming Childhood Trauma	£9.99	
	Overcoming Chronic Fatigue	£9.99	
	Overcoming Chronic Pain	£9.99	
	Overcoming Compulsive Gambling	£9.99	
	Overcoming Depression	£9.99	
	Overcoming Insomnia and Sleep Problems	£9.99	
	Overcoming Low Self-Esteem	£9.99	
	Overcoming Mood Swings	£9.99	
	Overcoming Obsessive Compulsive Disorders	£9.99	
	Overcoming Panic	£9.99	
	Overcoming Paranoid and Suspicious Thoughts	£9.99	
	Overcoming Problem Drinking	£9.99	
	Overcoming Relationship Problems	£9.99	
	Overcoming Sexual Problems	£9.99	
	Overcoming Social Anxiety and Shyness	£9.99	
	Overcoming Traumatic Stress	£9.99	
	Overcoming Weight Problems	£9.99	
	Overcoming Your Child's Fears and Worries	£9.99	
	Overcoming Your Smoking Habit	£9.99	
	P & P	FREE	
		Grand TOTAL £	

Name:

Delivery address:

Postcode:

Daytime tel. no.:

Email:

How to pay:

1. **By telephone**: call the TBS order line on 01206 522 800 and quote OSASHC. Phone lines are open between Monday – Friday, 8.30am – 5.30pm.

2. **By post**: send a cheque for the full amount payable to TBS Ltd. and send form to:
   Freepost RLUL-SJGC-SGKJ,
   Cash Sales/Direct Mail Dept.,
   The Book Service,
   Colchester Road, Frating,
   Colchester CO7 7DW